Lectionary Worship Aids

Cycle C, Series IV

James R. Wilson

CSS Publishing Company, Inc.
Lima, Ohio

LECTIONARY WORSHIP AIDS, SERIES IV, CYCLE C

Library of Congress Cataloging-in-Publication Data

Wilson, James R., 1943-
   Lectionary worship aids : Cycle A, Series IV / James R. Wilson.
       p.   cm.
   ISBN 0-7880-0548-0 - Cycle A
   1. Worship programs. 2. Gathering rites. 3. Church year. 4. Common lectionary (1992)
I. Title.
BV198.W55   1995
264'.13—dc20   95-14052
                                                                              CIP

Cycle B — ISBN 0-7880-0813-7
Cycle C — ISBN 0-7880-1024-7

This book is available in the following formats, listed by ISBN:
       0-7880-1024-7   Book
       0-7880-1025-5   Mac
       0-7880-1026-3   IBM 3 1/2
       0-7880-1083-2   Sermon Prep

PRINTED IN U.S.A.

It probably goes without saying that a work of this nature is first and foremost dedicated to our Lord and Savior Jesus Christ, without whose presence in my life it would never have been completed.

Others I would like to remember in dedicating this volume include my mother, who died in the summer of 1996 and whose love, wisdom and zest for life I will sorely miss; my very patient, understanding and supportive editor who has worked with me every step of the way through these three volumes; Bobbie, our friend in Christ, whose help and support has meant more than words can express; and my wife Jackie for her love and support over these past three years and who this year was appointed to two small churches of her own.

It really is true that no one prepares a work for the Lord in a vacuum, and as we come to the close of this three-volume effort my personal thoughts of appreciation overflow for each and every person who helped in their own special way to bring this work to completion. Collectively our prayer continues to be that what has been produced will in some way be a useful aid to church leaders intent on building rich and meaningful worship experiences.

May the Lord be with you.

Jim

Editor's Note Regarding The Lectionary

During the past two decades there has been an attempt to move in the direction of a uniform lectionary among various Protestant denominations.

Preaching on the same scripture lessons every Sunday is a step in the right direction of uniting Christians of many faiths. If we are reading the same scriptures together we may also begin to accomplish other achievements. Our efforts will be strengthened through our unity.

Beginning with Advent 1995 The Evangelical Lutheran Church in America dropped its own lectionary schedule and adopted the Revised Common Lectionary.

Reflecting this change, resources published by CSS Publishing Company put their major emphasis on the Revised Common Lectionary texts for the church year.

Table Of Contents

Introduction

It might be of some value to those who would use these materials to have some understanding of how they were constructed.

Purpose — It was never this author's intent to present a set of Calls to Worship and Prayers that would be considered definitive in nature. Instead, this work just seemed to grow out of the week in and week out efforts of trying to build worship services on the Revised Common Lectionary. Although these aids are intended to be "ready to use" as they are, it would also seem they might be helpful as creative "thought starters" for those who enjoy customizing their series to fit a specific worship event or congregation.

Format — The matter of format is a good bit more complicated. In their original form each of these services was created on a computer using about a 44 space line so as to fit the average bulletin page. Indentations from the left margin for the Collect and Prayer of Confession were set at 3 spaces and the textual indentation for the Call to Worship was set at 8 spaces. A hard spacing type font (a font that gives each letter the same spacing) was used (approximately a #10 Pica) rather than a proportional spacing font (a font that gives each letter a different size spacing according to the letter's shape) in order to provide a consistent line length.

Therefore, once the format is set up, each Call to Worship and Prayer should be the same line length. For those who are using memory printing equipment which allows you to edit rather than rewrite your bulletins every week, this should offer some obvious advantages. It also has some advantage in being able to plan the layout of the worship service to know exactly what line length each section is going to require.

Personal — And finally some personal thoughts. For anyone who has planned a worship experience and taken the task seriously, they will tell you this is not an easy assignment. Doing it once or several times every week can become an emotionally exhausting effort. But I believe genuine worship experiences are critical to the spiritual health and well-being of all Christians, our local congregations and the church universal. We all struggle to try to build meaningful services and if this work can help in any way to fulfill that task then let us join together and give thanks to the Lord.

— Jim Wilson

First Sunday In Advent

First Lesson: Jeremiah 33:14-16
Theme: The Promise

Call To Worship

Leader: Let all who seek the Lord enter this place for worship and praise!

People: We would know God's mercy and grace and we would hear God's holy word.

Leader: Each word spoken and each promise of God will stand forever.

People: Our God is faithful and true and we hear with joy the message of Christ.

Leader: Let our hearts be joined in praise and song before Almighty God.

All: Blessed be the name of the Lord!

Collect

Almighty and merciful God, You heard the cries of the ancients and sent us the Christ. Hear our cries today and renew our spirits in this season even as You did in the days of old. In Christ we pray. Amen.

Prayer Of Confession

Lord, so often as we enter the season of Advent we turn our attention toward all that must be done for the coming holidays and we fail to seek Your renewing presence in our lives. Forgive us, Lord. Come to us anew, restoring the joy in our hearts so that our lives might again be a witness to Your wonderful healing power and presence. In Christ we pray. Amen.

Hymns

"Come, Thou Almighty King"
"Abide With Me"
"Close To Thee"

First Sunday In Advent

Second Lesson: 1 Thessalonians 3:9-13
Theme: Growing in God's love

Call To Worship

Leader: The Lord is wonderful and mighty and is worthy of our love and praise!

People: And the Lord has blessed us and touched our lives with love.

Leader: As we love and care for one another we will be filled with God's joy.

People: And as we reach out and share God's love we will grow in Christ.

Leader: Let us join our voices this day in proclaiming the Good News of Christ!

All: Blessed be the name of the Lord!

Collect

O God, in Your infinite wisdom You call us to love one another so we might know the joy in life You intended for us to receive. Fill our hearts daily, Lord, with Your loving presence. In Christ we pray. Amen.

Prayer Of Confession

O God, again and again You have called us to love one another so that we might know Your blessings, but we have turned away each to our own ways. Too often, Lord, we have even focused our lives on meeting only our own wants, and we have failed to see and hear the needs of a hurting world around us. Forgive us, Lord, and fill our hearts with Your holy presence. In Christ we pray. Amen.

Hymns

"Love Divine, All Loves Excelling"
"Come, Thou Fount Of Every Blessing"
"Jesus Calls Us O'er The Tumult"

First Sunday In Advent

Gospel: Luke 21:25-36
Theme: Living prepared!

Call To Worship

Leader: Show us Your mercy, O Lord. Send us a sign of Your presence and love.

People: Grant us Your salvation, Lord, for we are weary and worn.

Leader: The Lord's Truth shall indeed be among us.

People: God's Righteousness shall come from heaven to be in our midst.

Leader: And there shall be peace to all who turn to God in their hearts.

All: Blessed be the name of the Lord!

Collect

Almighty and merciful God, in the words of Christ You have called us always to be alert and true to Your call on our lives, for we have no guarantee of tomorrow. We praise You, O God. In Christ we pray. Amen.

Prayer Of Confession

Lord, so often we have been like those of old who waited for You to send a Savior. We have prayed for You to deliver us from our circumstances, but we have not been willing to accept Your leadership in our lives. Forgive us, Lord, for not seeing Your presence around us and for acting at times like Jesus did not die for our sins. In Christ we pray. Amen.

Hymns

"Forward Through The Ages"
"Come, Christians, Join In Song"
"Living For Jesus"

Second Sunday In Advent

First Lesson: Malachi 3:1-4
Theme: The cleansing of the Lord

Call To Worship

Leader: Come, let the people of God give praise and worship the Lord!

People: For the Lord has shown us the ways of righteousness and love.

Leader: And through Christ we have been washed clean of our sins.

People: Like fine gold the Lord brings us through the fires of cleansing.

Leader: Let us sing and praise the Lord God Almighty in whom is our salvation.

All: Blessed be the name of the Lord!

Collect

Almighty God, You alone could justly have destroyed us for our iniquities, yet in Your mercy and love You sent the Christ both to reveal justice and to die so that we might truly have life. In Christ we pray. Amen.

Prayer Of Confession

Lord, so often we have taken for granted the wonderful blessing of your mercy and grace. Too often we have acted as though we deserved Your forgiveness instead of Your wrath. Forgive us, Lord, and help us to see in the life of Jesus how badly we have each fallen short of what You created us to be. Give us the strength and courage to live for You. In Christ we pray. Amen.

Hymns

"Grace Greater Than All Our Sin"
"There Is A Fountain Filled With Blood"
"Would You Live For Jesus"

Second Sunday In Advent

Second Lesson: Philippians 1:3-11
Theme: Living the Gospel of Christ

Call To Worship

Leader: Let us worship the Lord God Almighty with every breath of our lives.

People: Let the love of Christ shine through all that we do or say.

Leader: For it is Christ who has given us joy and wisdom and insight.

People: Christ died that we might have life even before we realized our sins.

Leader: Then let our voices be raised in praise for the life we have been given.

All: Blessed be the name of the Lord!

Collect

Most wonderful and loving God, You not only call us to be a part of Your family but, through the gift of Your Holy Spirit, You also empower us to be Your living witnesses. We praise You, Lord. In Christ we pray. Amen.

Prayer Of Confession

Lord, we have taken for granted the wonderful gift of Your grace and mercy. We have been so involved with our lives that we have refused to allow You to use us so we might become a blessing to others. Forgive us, Lord, and give us the strength and courage to risk all that we are in order that we might be living witnesses for You. In Christ we pray. Amen.

Hymns

"On Christ The Solid Rock I Stand"
"I Stand Amazed In The Presence"
"Living For Jesus"

Second Sunday In Advent

Gospel: Luke 3:1-6
Theme: Prepare the way of the Lord

Call To Worship

Leader: Let us all give praise before the Lord with gladness and joy.

People: This is our God, on whom we have waited for our salvation.

Leader: For the Lord is near to all who call out to God in love and truth.

People: The Lord is indeed our Help and the Holy One who delivers us.

Leader: Let us shout the message for all to hear of God's mercy and grace.

All: Blessed be the name of the Lord!

Collect

Most gracious and loving Lord, in Your infinite wisdom You call us to proclaim the wonderful news of Christ to all the nations and we will be blessed. We give You our praise, dear Lord. In Christ we pray. Amen.

Prayer Of Confession

Lord, in so many ways You have sent us the message of Your salvation, yet we have been too busy to hear. In so many ways, even through the Christ, You have tried to show us Your Love, but we would not see. And so often You would have us share Your Love with others that You might bless the world through us, but we would not share it. Forgive us, Lord. In Christ we pray. Amen.

Hymns

"We've A Story To Tell To The Nations"
"Hallelujah! What A Savior"
"Jesus Is All The World To Me"

14

Third Sunday In Advent

First Lesson: Zephaniah 3:14-20
Theme: The Blessing of the Lord

Call To Worship

Leader: Let all of God's children stand firm and give witness in the world!

People: For the Lord is our salvation and our strength before all nations.

Leader: It has always been the Lord who has sustained us even in the hard times.

People: The world has seen our deepest joy giving witness to God's Love.

Leader: Let us celebrate and lift our voices together in praise.

All: Blessed be the name of the Lord!

Collect

Almighty and everlasting God, You hold us safe and sure in Your magnificent right hand. In Your infinite grace and mercy, You have sustained us and called us Your own. We praise You, O Lord. In Christ we pray. Amen.

Prayer Of Confession

Lord, so often we think of ourselves as independent and self-sustaining people and we have failed to confess Your blessings and presence in our lives. We even forget that it is You who sustains the universe itself, of which we are only a tiny part. Forgive us, Lord, and help us soar with the eagles as we rest our wings on Your sustaining love. In Christ we pray. Amen.

Hymns

"To God Be The Glory, Great Things He Has Done"
"How Great Thou Art"
"Leaning On The Everlasting Arms"

Third Sunday In Advent

Second Lesson: Philippians 4:4-7
Theme: Rejoice in the Lord

Call To Worship

Leader: Come! Rejoice! Let our praises ring out for all the world to hear!

People: Praise be to God who is our Lord and our only salvation.

Leader: The Lord has sustained and cared for us and is our most loving parent.

People: Let our hearts be open before the Lord, for God hears our every prayer.

Leader: Let us rejoice, for in Christ we have been given God's greatest blessing.

All: Blessed be the name of the Lord!

Collect

Most gracious and merciful Lord, in Your loving way You stand ready to bless us as we serve You so that we might proclaim Your wonder and greatness for all to hear. We praise Your holy name, Lord. In Christ we pray. Amen.

Prayer Of Confession

Lord, You have given us so much to rejoice about, yet we have only complained and sought more. So often in our desires for more we have also failed to proclaim to the world the blessings and joy You have already made possible for us through Christ and the cross. Forgive us, Lord, and give us the vision to see Your presence and rejoice in it. In Christ we pray. Amen.

Hymns

"Rejoice, Ye Pure In Heart"
"Praise Him! Praise Him!"
"Savior, Like A Shepherd Lead Us"

Third Sunday In Advent

Gospel: Luke 3:7-18
Theme: Waiting upon the Lord

Call To Worship

Leader: Wait upon the Lord! Be strong and let your hearts take courage!

People: We do wait upon God's promise and healing power in the world today.

Leader: Wait upon the Lord! Be strong and let your hearts take courage!

People: Teach us Your ways, O Lord, and lead us to follow Your paths.

Leader: Wait upon the Lord! Be strong and let your hearts sing praise!

All: Blessed be the name of the Lord!

Collect

Most gracious and merciful Lord, through the prophets of old and through the words of Christ and the Scriptures, You call us to live that love You first extended to us so that all may see it in us. Praise You, Lord. In Christ we pray. Amen.

Prayer Of Confession

Lord, as we continue our journey toward Christmas, we are so aware, there is much in the world to deafen our ears to the sound of angel anthems or to blind our eyes to the star that would guide us to the manger. Lord, forgive us when we let the world distract us from Your Love or from sharing it with others. Help us focus our hearts on You. In Christ we pray. Amen.

Hymns

"O Come, O Come, Emmanuel"
"Lift Up Your Heads, Ye Mighty Gates"
"I Want To Walk As A Child Of The Light"

Fourth Sunday In Advent

First Lesson: Micah 5:2-5a
Theme: The Savior is coming

Call To Worship

Leader: Come now and know the presence of the Lord God of Hosts!

People: We once pleaded for God to send us a Savior to lead us into life.

Leader: And God heard our plea and sent the Christ to be our salvation.

People: From the humblest of beginnings the Lord lifted up our Savior.

Leader: For the world would not hear the words of the prophets of old.

All: Blessed be the name of the Lord!

Collect

Almighty and merciful God, in Your infinite wisdom You raised up our Messiah from the ranks of the humble and lowly, not from the ranks of the powerful and famous. We praise You, O God. In Christ we pray. Amen.

Prayer Of Confession

O Lord, even though we know You were born in humble circumstances and Your life and teachings proclaimed the importance of using all that we are and have to serve You and others, we have instead sought to focus on bettering only our own lives and situations. Forgive us, Lord, and restore our spirits, that we might once again be Your faithful servants. In Christ we pray. Amen.

Hymns

"O Little Town Of Bethlehem"
"Savior Of The Nations, Come"
"Others"

Fourth Sunday In Advent

Second Lesson: Hebrews 10:5-10
Theme: Christ, our Sacrifice for salvation

Call To Worship

Leader: Come, let all of God's people give praise and worship the Lord!

People: For we were once lost and without hope before the Lord God Almighty.

Leader: On the cross the price was paid for our sins for all who accept Christ.

People: In Christ we are washed clean before God of stains we could not remove.

Leader: Then let us celebrate and give praise and lift our voices in joyful song.

All: Blessed be the name of the Lord!

Collect

Merciful and eternal God, You saw our sins and knew that we could not atone for them. So You sent the Christ to die in our place that we might have life everlasting. We give You our lives, Lord. In Christ we pray. Amen.

Prayer Of Confession

Lord, so often we have forgotten the price You paid for us on the cross. We have even allowed ourselves to believe we may be worthy of the grace and mercy You have shown us. Forgive us, Lord, and once again help us to see ourselves and our sins as You see us, that we might realize the enormous debt we owe You and be more ready to share Your love with others. In Christ we pray. Amen.

Hymns

"My Hope Is Built On Nothing Less"
"Jesus, Keep Me Near The Cross"
"Jesus Paid It All"

Fourth Sunday In Advent

Gospel: Luke 1:39-45 (46-55)
Theme: God's promise fulfilled

Call To Worship

Leader: Come! Let us celebrate, for the Lord has heard our cries!

People: Our Savior is coming; the Kingdom of God is at hand.

Leader: The sick and the lame shall be healed and no longer despised.

People: The poor and the afflicted will be vindicated and inherit the Kingdom.

Leader: Let us raise our voices for all to hear, "The Savior is coming!"

All: Blessed be the name of the Lord!

Collect

Most wonderful and loving God, You heard our pleas for a Savior and just as it was written, through the womb of a virgin, You sent us the Christ. With all of our love we give You our praise. In Christ we pray. Amen.

Prayer Of Confession

Lord, so often we have lifted our voices in cries for help, yet we have failed to prepare our hearts to receive You. Too often we have called for Your justice and pleaded for vindication, but we would not hear Your personal call on our lives. We have not been obedient children, yet You love us still. Forgive us, Lord, and help us to prepare for You today. In Christ we pray. Amen.

Hymns

"There's A Song In The Air"
"It Came Upon The Midnight Clear"
"Abide With Me"

Christmas Day

First Lesson: Isaiah 52:7-10
Theme: The Lord has come!

Call To Worship

Leader: Come, let us celebrate, for Christ our Savior has been born!

People: **Is our Messiah, the promised one, among us this day?**

Leader: Surely I say unto you, Christ the Lord is with us even as we speak.

People: **Are even sinners such as we welcome in Christ's kingdom?**

Leader: Praise to the Lord God Almighty, for in Christ we are all welcome!

All: **Blessed be the name of the Lord!**

Collect

O God, You have answered our prayers and through the gift of Your Son You have given us a Savior. O Lord, lead us to share this most wonderful gift with all the world. In Christ we pray. Amen.

Prayer Of Confession

Lord, so often we have allowed the worldly trappings of the holidays to blur our vision and pull us away from the true message of Christmas. Forgive us, Lord, and where we find the hurting, let us give comfort; where we see need, let us give a helping hand; and where we find the lost, give us the wisdom and courage to lead them home to You. In Christ we pray. Amen.

Hymns

"Angels We Have Heard On High"
"Good Christian Friends, Rejoice"
"O Come, All Ye Faithful"

Christmas Day

Second Lesson: Hebrews 1:1-4 (5-12)
Theme: Praise be to God, our Savior has come

Call To Worship

Leader: Let our voices be lifted together in song and celebration!

People: For what good news do we celebrate on this day?

Leader: Let us join the angelic hosts in praising God, for Christ is born!

People: Praise to God the Almighty for hearing our prayers for salvation.

Leader: Let our hearts be joined in praise as we lift our voices in song!

All: Blessed be the name of the Lord!

Collect

O Lord, as we pause to consider the magnitude of the blessing of Christmas, we are left humble and overwhelmed. Just now we lift to You our deepest heartfelt love and praise. In Christ we pray. Amen.

Prayer Of Confession

Lord, so often we have heard the story of Christmas, yet we hardly take the time to hear the message of Your love it proclaims. So often, Lord, we have been more concerned with our programs and decorations than the wonderful news of personal mercy and grace Christmas calls us to hear. Forgive us, Lord, and fill our hearts with love. In Christ we pray. Amen.

Hymns

"O Come, All Ye Faithful"
"Away In A Manger"
"Sing We Now Of Christmas"

Christmas Day

Gospel: John 1:1-14
Theme: The Word of God is with us

Call To Worship

Leader: Let us gather together and give praise, for God's Word has come.

People: The Word of the Lord was sent that we might all know of God's love.

Leader: Yet the world would not hear and it turned away from the Word.

People: But we have heard the Word and its truth has touched our hearts.

Leader: Then let our hearts proclaim the Word for all the world to hear!

All: Blessed be the name of the Lord!

Collect

O God, our words are hardly adequate to proclaim the message of love Christ came to share with us. Hear our prayer, O Lord; we lift our hearts before you in praise and thanksgiving. In Christ we pray. Amen.

Prayer Of Confession

O God, You have shown us Your love through the gift of Your Word. Forgive us, God, for all of those times when we have grieved You by not accepting Your Word; or by not passing Your Word along and loving one another. Forgive our selfishness and intolerance, Lord. Heal our hearts that we might grow into the loving witnesses You would have us be. In Christ we pray. Amen.

Hymns

"O Come, All Ye Faithful"
"Silent Night"
"Joy To The World"

First Sunday After Christmas

First Lesson: 1 Samuel 2:18-20, 26
Theme: Dedication to the Lord

Call To Worship

Leader: Let all who are dedicated to serving the Lord come together for worship!

People: We bring praise and wonder in our hearts for God's forgiving love.

Leader: Yet we are called to dedicate our total lives to the service of Christ.

People: Gladly we walk with Christ, for each day we grow in love and wisdom.

Leader: Then let us loudly proclaim the joy and wonder of God's love.

All: Blessed be the name of the Lord!

Collect

O God, Your wisdom surpasses all that we could imagine, and in the wonder of Your love You have chosen to walk with us and guide us as we dedicate our hearts and lives to You. We praise You, Lord. In Christ we pray. Amen.

Prayer Of Confession

Lord, in our inflated view of our own wisdom we feel we know more about what is best for us and those around us than do You who created and understands the Universe itself. We have even told You what would be best in our lives. Forgive us, Lord, and help us to have the faith and courage to submit our wills to Your holy will. In Christ we pray. Amen.

Hymns

"My Hope Is Built On Nothing Less"
"Are Ye Able?"
"O Master, Let Me Walk With Thee"

First Sunday After Christmas

Second Lesson: Colossians 3:12-17
Theme: Living Christ's love

Call To Worship

Leader: Great and wonderful are Your works, O Lord!

People: In the mountains and the hills we are in awe of Your majesty.

Leader: In the heavens above we sense the vastness of Your Creation.

People: In the winds and the storms we know You are the Almighty God.

Leader: In the gift of our Savior, we know You are Love.

All: Blessed be the name of the Lord!

Collect

Almighty and merciful God, in Your infinite strength You extend to us Your gentle forgiveness and grace. Lord, help us to use our strength to extend mercy and grace to others. In Christ we pray. Amen.

Prayer Of Confession

Lord, in this season of giving gifts, somehow we let ourselves overlook the greatest gift of all, our Savior. We would be busy exchanging or complaining and miss completely the peace and love You came to give us. Forgive us, Lord, for we have been unappreciative children. Touch our hearts anew with the true glory and wonder that is Christmas. In Christ we pray. Amen.

Hymns

"Love Came Down At Christmas"
"Go, Tell It On The Mountain"
"I Heard The Bells On Christmas Day"

First Sunday After Christmas

Gospel: Luke 2:41-52
Theme: Jesus, God with us

Call To Worship

Leader: Let us enter God's house this day to praise and worship the Lord!

People: God heard our pleas and in Jesus came sharing the joy of divine love.

Leader: In Jesus we saw God with us and the world would not hear his word.

People: God's wisdom confounds even the wise among us, yet God loves us each one.

Leader: Then let us celebrate with joyful hearts the wonderful gift of Christ.

All: Blessed be the name of the Lord!

Collect

Almighty God, Creator and Sustainer of all the universe, in the life and words of Jesus Your wisdom and love challenged all that we had come to believe. Help us now to share Your love. In Christ we pray. Amen.

Prayer Of Confession

O God, so often we have thought too highly of the wisdom by which we have chosen to live, and we have failed to seek Your wisdom and Your guidance in our lives. When we have prayed seeking Your guidance, too often we have still chosen to ignore Your will and go our own ways. Forgive us, Lord, and give us the strength and courage to seek and follow You. In Christ we pray. Amen.

Hymns

"I Wonder As I Wander"
"What Child Is This?"
"Sweet Hour Of Prayer"

January 1
(New Year's Day Alternate Service)

Scripture: Isaiah 6:1-8
Theme: Service of Recommitment to Christian Service for the New Year

Call To Worship

Leader: Come, let all who love the Lord gather in this house for worship!

People: And let all who have heard the Gospel of Christ celebrate.

Leader: But there are some who have heard and turned away.

People: And some who have never heard the Good News Christ came to share.

Leader: Then let us recommit our lives to sharing the Gospel for all to hear.

All: Blessed be the name of the Lord!

Collect

O Lord, we come before You just now accepting the responsibilities You would place upon us as part of Your church today and asking You to walk with us and lead us in all that we do. In Christ we pray. Amen.

Prayer Of Confession

Lord, all too many times we have taken the role of being Your church in today's world too lightly. So often we have allowed so many things to come before our duty to You and to the church. Forgive us, Lord, and make us more sensitive to Your leading, that our lives might once again be a strong and unclouded witness for You. In Christ we pray. Amen.

Hymns

"Ask Ye What Great Thing I Know"
"We've A Story To Tell To The Nations"
"Go, Make Of All Disciples"

Second Sunday After Christmas

First Lesson: Jeremiah 31:7-14
Theme: In all seasons have faith

Call To Worship

Leader: Come, let all who worship the Lord gather to sing and hear the Word!

People: But our days have been hard and our spirits are near broken.

Leader: But the Lord God Almighty will deliver and keep you as God's own.

People: But times have been so hard, as though God has forgotten us.

Leader: Fear not, for the Lord your God is come and God's kingdom is at hand.

All: Blessed be the name of the Lord!

Collect

O God, in all of these times when life is so difficult, help us to remember Your promise always to be with us and to be our strength whenever we will walk in the ways of Your leading. In Christ we pray. Amen.

Prayer Of Confession

O God, so often when life has been hard and situations have seemed impossible, we have turned away from the hope You would give us and chosen instead despair and sorrow. Too often, Lord, if things were unlikely by the world's standards, we would not believe. Forgive us, Lord, and help us always to lean on Your wisdom and strength as our hope. In Christ we pray. Amen.

Hymns

"Ring The Bells"
"I Know Whom I Have Believed"
"Grace That Is Greater Than All Our Sin"

Second Sunday After Christmas

Second Lesson: Ephesians 1:3-14
Theme: The New Covenant

Call To Worship

Leader: Let any who would know the living Christ come and worship this day!

People: But may we as sinners enter into the house of the Lord?

Leader: In the Blood of Christ came the New Covenant. Even sinners may enter!

People: But how can sinners enter into the house of Almighty God?

Leader: In Christ, God has washed away our sin and made us each one clean.

All: Blessed be the name of the Lord!

Collect

O God, in Christ You have given us a New Covenant, calling to us to come home just as the Good Shepherd lovingly calls in the sheep. Give us the wisdom to follow You, Lord. In Christ we pray. Amen.

Prayer Of Confession

God, so often we have sought to earn Your mercy and grace and have refused to accept them as the gifts of love You intend them to be. So often in our pride we will not receive that which we have not earned. Forgive us, Lord, and help us to understand we must freely accept Your gifts in order that we might freely share them and pass them on to others. In Christ we pray. Amen.

Hymns

"I Will Sing The Wondrous Story"
"Sing We Now Of Christmas"
"Freely, Freely"

Second Sunday After Christmas

Gospel: John 1:(1-9) 10-18
Theme: The Word dwelt among us

Call To Worship

Leader: Come, all who would bear witness of the Word, let us worship!

People: For the Word was made flesh and dwelt among us; Jesus was the Word.

Leader: And in Christ we were made whole and brought in the presence of God.

People: For the witness of Christ was of God, that all should know the Lord.

Leader: So let us lift our voices in song and praise, for God so loved us all.

All: Blessed be the name of the Lord!

Collect

O God, through the giving of the Word become flesh in Christ, You have spoken to us of unlimited accepting love. Help us to have the courage to receive Your gift and share it. In Christ we pray. Amen.

Prayer Of Confession

O God, sometimes we are so overwhelmed by the universe we are willing to believe You are so incomprehensible we would never be able to know You. Forgive us, Lord, when we refuse to see that You loved and wanted to know us so much You sent Jesus, that we might hear and accept Your Word. Open our eyes to Your love, Lord, that we might walk with You daily. In Christ we pray. Amen.

Hymns

"That Boy-Child Of Mary"
"Blessed Assurance"
"O Come And Dwell In Me"

Epiphany

First Lesson: Isaiah 60:1-6
Theme: The Light has come

Call To Worship

Leader: Come, let all of God's people give praise and worship the Lord!

People: For we were once in darkness but God has sent us the Light.

Leader: And we are to take God's Light into all of the world,

People: That others should no longer be in darkness but receive God's Light.

Leader: Let us celebrate our mission and let us always give God the praise.

All: Blessed be the name of the Lord!

Collect

O God, we are so grateful You have opened the door for us to be a part of Your kingdom and ministry in our world today. Soften our hearts that You might use us freely. In Christ we pray. Amen.

Prayer Of Confession

Lord, so often we have taken for granted the wonderful mission You gave each one of us as we became a part of Your church. Too often our days have returned to the mundane and we have lost sight of our commission to take Your Light into the darkness wherever we find it. Forgive us, Lord, and restore our passion to serve and live for You. In Christ we pray. Amen.

Hymns

"Let There Be Peace On Earth"
"I Want To Walk As A Child Of Light"
"Be Thou My Vision"

Epiphany

Second Lesson: Ephesians 3:1-12
Theme: One Kingdom established by Christ

Call To Worship

Leader: Come! Let the believers from every nation gather to worship the Lord.

People: Are all nations welcome in the house of the Lord?

Leader: In Christ, all peoples from every nation are made welcome!

People: Are there not Jew and Gentile, each in their own place?

Leader: In Christ there is no east or west and all peoples are beloved of God.

All: Blessed be the name of the Lord!

Collect

O God, in Christ You gave us such a wonderful blessing as You taught us to love and to accept others and not the ways of hatred and division. Give us the strength to follow You, Lord. In Christ we pray. Amen.

Prayer Of Confession

O God, so often we have chosen to follow the ways of the world as we look at others who are different from ourselves and deep in our hearts we fail to love and accept them. Lord, forgive us and help us to reach out and accept others and realize we are all Your children for whom Jesus died on the cross so we might each one know God's love. In Christ we pray. Amen.

Hymns

"Creator Of The Earth And Skies"
"I Love Thy Kingdom, Lord"
"God Will Take Care Of You"

Epiphany

Gospel: Matthew 2:1-12
Theme: The Incarnation

Call To Worship

Leader: Come, let us know the Lord God Almighty is present this day!

People: **We heard the Good News in the birth of our Lord.**

Leader: Even the stars in the heavens announced the birth of Christ.

People: **Christ was sent that we might all know of God's Love and grace.**

Leader: Then let us proclaim the birth of Christ for all the world to hear!

All: **Blessed be the name of the Lord!**

Collect

O God, You have called us to spread Your Gospel in the world today. In Christ, You showed us in that single life the Love You meant for us to share. Help us share it, Lord. In Christ we pray. Amen.

Prayer Of Confession

Lord, so often amid the rush and turmoil of the season we hear the glory of Your birth and we take it for granted. Too often we hear of the miracle of Your coming and we hardly slow down to take notice. Forgive us, Lord, and touch our hearts today with the true meaning of Your birth that we might proclaim it in all the world. In Christ we pray. Amen.

Hymns

"He Is Lord"
"Tell Me The Story Of Jesus"
"Jesus, Lover Of My Soul"

Baptism Of Our Lord

First Lesson: Isaiah 43:1-7
Theme: The Lord is our salvation

Call To Worship

Leader: Come, let all of God's people gather this day for worship!
People: **For we were once lost and without hope until the Lord redeemed us.**
Leader: Even when we were yet in our sin Christ died that we might have life.
People: **We have salvation only through the mercy and grace of our Lord.**
Leader: Then let our hearts proclaim God's redeeming love for all nations to hear.
All: **Blessed be the name of the Lord!**

Collect

Almighty and loving Lord, in Your divine wisdom You knew we needed salvation even when we were yet lost and determined to go our own way. We praise You, O Lord, for Your loving mercy and grace. In Christ we pray. Amen.

Prayer Of Confession

Lord, we have sought our salvation in every other direction rather than turning to You. We have even thought the temporal world and its honors and glory and fame would fill our need for Your presence in our hearts and lives. Forgive us, Lord, and hear the prayers of our hearts today as we once again turn our lives back to You. In Christ we pray. Amen.

Hymns

"All Hail The Power Of Jesus' Name"
"Praise To The Lord, The Almighty"
"Amazing Grace"

Baptism Of Our Lord

Second Lesson: Acts 8:14-17
Theme: Receiving God's Holy Spirit

Call To Worship

Leader: Let all who would seek God's presence gather now for worship!

People: We desire in our hearts the joy and wonder of the Holy Spirit.

Leader: In our commitment to Christ we are promised the gift of the Helper.

People: Then let our lives be touched and our hearts healed by God's love.

Leader: And let us open our hearts and let the Holy Spirit touch and heal us.

All: Blessed be the name of the Lord!

Collect

O God, in Your infinite wisdom You knew we would need a Helper to guide us in the paths of righteousness. We thank You, O Lord, and ask that You give us the courage to follow, no matter the price. In Christ we pray. Amen.

Prayer Of Confession

Lord, too often we have been so involved in the daily matters around us that we have lost sight of the wonderful gift You have given us in the guidance and leadership of the Holy Spirit. Forgive us, O Lord, and once again lead us in the paths You would call us to go so that we might carry the Good News of Christ for all peoples and nations to hear. In Christ we pray. Amen.

Hymns

"Lead On, O King Eternal"
"Leaning On Jesus"
"Abide With Me"

Baptism Of Our Lord

Gospel: Luke 3:15-17, 21-22
Theme: Our Baptism, a call to serve

Call To Worship

Leader: Come all who would hear the call to proclaim God's prophetic word.

People: We are called to take light where there was darkness and despair.

Leader: We are called to carry hope to lives where hope has been lost.

People: We are called to share God's love so all might know true life itself.

Leader: We are called to proclaim God's mercy and grace for all to hear.

All: Blessed be the name of the Lord!

Collect

Most wonderful and loving God, in the life of Jesus You showed us the kind of love You would have us share with the world. Help us remember our baptism, Lord, that we might serve others for You. In Christ we pray. Amen.

Prayer Of Confession

Lord, so often we have completely ignored the prophetic tasks You would have us be doing in today's world. We have been too busy with our daily lives to share Your Word around us. And we have been timid and afraid before the opinions of others. Forgive us, Lord, and give us the courage to witness boldly of Your love today. In Christ we pray. Amen.

Hymns

"Marching To Zion"
"Pass It On"
"Others"

Second Sunday After Epiphany

First Lesson: Isaiah 62:1-5
Theme: God's promise of greatness

Call To Worship

Leader: Come, let all of God's people give praise and worship the Lord!

People: For in Christ we are heirs to the Kingdom of God.

Leader: For the children of God will see lifted up for all nations to see.

People: Let us proclaim the glory of God that all might hear and be saved.

Leader: Let our hearts and our voices be joined in praise to Almighty God.

All: Blessed be the name of the Lord!

Collect

Almighty and wonderful God, according to Your divine will, You call us to be witnesses of Your loving and merciful grace before the nations of the world. We thank You and give You our praise, Lord. In Christ we pray. Amen.

Prayer Of Confession

O God, we have often let ourselves believe in our hearts that somehow we actually deserve Your mercy and Your grace in our lives. Too often we have even proclaimed to the world more of our pride and self-righteousness than we have of the forgiveness and grace we have received. Forgive us, Lord, and help us to proclaim Your Good News. In Christ we pray. Amen.

Hymns

"Love, Mercy, And Grace"
"Immortal, Invisible, God Only Wise"
"We've A Story To Tell To The Nations"

Second Sunday After Epiphany

Second Lesson: 1 Corinthians 12:1-11
Theme: Prepared for service

Call To Worship

Leader: Let God's people gather this day in worship and song before the Lord!

People: For the Lord is holy and gives to each the gifts for service.

Leader: Then let us use our gifts freely to serve our Lord and Savior.

People: Let the redeeming light of Christ be shined in the darkness of the world.

Leader: Let us celebrate together and serve Christ with all we have been given.

All: Blessed be the name of the Lord!

Collect

Almighty and most gracious God, You have called us to service and have even provided for us all we would need in order to serve through the presence of Your Holy Spirit. We praise You, O Lord. In Christ we pray. Amen.

Prayer Of Confession

O God, You have called us to be Your children and empowered us to be witnesses of Your mercy and grace, yet so often we have each one turned to our own ways and used Your gifts for our own interests. Forgive us, O Lord, and once again touch us with Your Holy Spirit. Call us again to service that others might hear the wonderful news of salvation. In Christ we pray. Amen.

Hymns

"Blessed Assurance"
"He Touched Me"
"My Hope Is Built On Nothing Less"

Second Sunday After Epiphany

Gospel: John 2:1-11
Theme: In Christ we are given true life

Call To Worship

Leader: Let all who have known the mercy of the Lord come together!

People: Through God's grace, the house of the Lord is open to each of us.

Leader: Yet we come as sinners, each fallen short of what God created us to be.

People: But in Christ, truly each of us is beloved in the eyes of God.

Leader: Then let our praise be heard for the mercy and grace of God.

All: Blessed be the name of the Lord!

Collect

O God, in Your infinite wisdom You sent us the Christ that we might have true life and know the joy Your presence brings in our hearts. We thank You, dear Lord, and we give You our praise. In Christ we pray. Amen.

Prayer Of Confession

Lord, so often we tend to come before You as if we deserve Your grace and mercy. So often we tend to act as if among all of Your people, we alone deserve Your favor. And too often we seem to either ignore our own sin or we focus too much on it, and we fail to see and receive the joy of life in Christ You intended for us to have. Forgive us, Lord. In Christ we pray. Amen.

Hymns

"All Hail The Power Of Jesus' Name"
"Love Divine, All Loves Excelling"
"He Lifted Me"

Third Sunday After Epiphany

First Lesson: Nehemiah 8:1-3, 5-6, 8-10
Theme: The joy of the Lord is our strength

Call To Worship

Leader: Give praise to the Lord and let our voices be lifted in joyful song!

People: For the Lord is our strength and our salvation.

Leader: We were once lost and without hope as sinners before our righteous God.

People: Yet in Christ we have been washed clean and given joy in our souls.

Leader: Then let us celebrate the wonder and grace of our almighty and merciful God.

All: Blessed be the name of the Lord!

Collect

O God, Creator and Sustainer of us all, in Your infinite wisdom You knew we needed Your salvation, hope, and joy if we were to be all You created us to be. We praise Your loving kindness, Lord. In Christ we pray. Amen.

Prayer Of Confession

Lord, we have chased after everything the world has to offer thinking we would find peace, hope, and joy, only to experience again and again that the world alone cannot meet the needs of our spirit. Forgive us, Lord, and touch us anew with Your healing love so we might celebrate once again the joy of life only Your presence with us can give. In Christ we pray. Amen.

Hymns

"Joyful, Joyful, We Adore Thee"
"Rejoice, Ye Pure In Heart"
"His Way With Thee"

Third Sunday After Epiphany

Second Lesson: 1 Corinthians 12:12-31a
Theme: Together we are Christ's Church

Call To Worship

Leader: We are one in the Spirit; we are one in the love of our Lord.

People: But we all have such differing backgrounds and varying needs.

Leader: Yet together in Christ we know a oneness that reflects God's love.

People: A oneness that calls us to share a joy about life with all we meet.

Leader: Then let our lives proclaim the oneness of Christ for all to see!

All: Blessed be the name of the Lord!

Collect

O merciful and loving God, through Your Holy Spirit You call us to service and You provide us the gifts to carry out Your call in concert as Your Church. We praise Your gracious wisdom, Lord. In Christ we pray. Amen.

Prayer Of Confession

Lord, we have often let our focus in life become too narrow. We tend to see only the events in our own lives, our own church, our own denomination, or even our own country, and we have lost sight of Your call for us to witness to the whole world. Too often, Lord, we have forgotten to be the Family of God You called us to be. Forgive us, Lord. In Christ we pray. Amen.

Hymns

"Filled With The Spirit's Power"
"I Am Thine, O Lord"
"O Jesus, I Have Promised"

Third Sunday After Epiphany

Gospel: Luke 4:14-21
Theme: Proclaim the Word of the Lord

Call To Worship

Leader: Come, all who would hear the call to proclaim the Word of the Lord!

People: We are called to take God's Word into a world burdened with despair.

Leader: And we are called to share hope in lives that seem hopeless and lost.

People: Let us share God's love with all we meet so all might have hope again.

Leader: Let us proclaim the Gospel of Christ in every nation and every land.

All: Blessed be the name of the Lord!

Collect

Almighty and wonderful Lord, in Your mercy and grace You allow us to be a part of carrying the Good News of Christ into all the world. We thank You and give You our praise. In Christ we pray. Amen.

Prayer Of Confession

Lord, so often we have allowed the demands of daily life to be so important to us that we have forgotten to share Your Word with others. We have even been so busy that we have not come to You ourselves and we have let the hopelessness of the world drain away the hope You gave us. Forgive us, Lord, and give us the courage to speak out boldly of Your love. In Christ we pray. Amen.

Hymns

"Ask Ye What Great Thing I Know"
"Pass It On"
"Take My Life And Let It Be"

Fourth Sunday After Epiphany

First Lesson: Jeremiah 1:4-10
Theme: The Lord is our strength

Call To Worship

Leader: Let all who would serve the Lord enter God's house for worship!

People: We would serve the Lord our God but we are weak and without voice.

Leader: The Lord is our strength and gives us the words to proclaim to all.

People: Then let us lean upon the Lord and lift our voices to serve the Christ.

Leader: And let our hearts be not afraid as we proclaim the Word of the Lord.

All: Blessed be the name of the Lord!

Collect

Almighty Creator God, You have called us to go forth in faith with Your promise to be our strength and our guide. Give us the courage, Lord, to proclaim Your Word boldly. We thank You, Lord. In Christ we pray. Amen.

Prayer Of Confession

Lord, so often we have heard Your call for us to proclaim the Good News of Christ wherever we are, yet we have held back for fear of not knowing what to say. Too often we have been more concerned about what others might think than we have been about being faithful to You. Forgive us, Lord, and fill us with Your Word to share with the world. In Christ we pray. Amen.

Hymns

"Victory In Jesus"
"Take My Life And Let It Be"
"Only Trust Him"

Fourth Sunday After Epiphany

Second Lesson: 1 Corinthians 13:1-13
Theme: Committing to love God's way

Call To Worship

Leader: We come together in Christ to live and share God's love in the world.

People: We come together to bring patience into a world full of impatience;

Leader: To bring understanding and concern where there is darkness and pain;

People: And to bring strength and courage that we may all grow in the Lord.

Leader: We do all this because God first loved us through Jesus our Savior.

All: Blessed be the name of the Lord!

Collect

Almighty and merciful God, in Your divine wisdom You have empowered us through Your Holy Spirit to carry Your agape love into the world. Use us, Lord, in every path we walk to love others. In Christ we pray. Amen.

Prayer Of Confession

Lord, we have often misunderstood our personal attractions to others as reaching out to share the unconditional love You would have us live today. Instead of loving, we have often turned away from those not like us whom You died on the Cross to save. Forgive us, Lord, and help us have the spiritual vision to see and love others as You do. In Christ we pray. Amen.

Hymns

"Love Divine, All Loves Excelling"
"In Christ There Is No East Or West"
"The Gift Of Love"

Fourth Sunday After Epiphany

Gospel: Luke 4:21-30
Theme: Familiarity versus Faith

Call To Worship

Leader: Come, let all who would proclaim the glory of God enter now for worship!

People: The Lord is our shepherd, in whom we rest our lives and our salvation.

Leader: Then let our voices be raised in praise and worship for all to hear.

People: But some who know us well wonder how we as sinners can worship Christ.

Leader: Let the wonder of God's grace and mercy in Christ be shared with all.

All: Blessed be the name of the Lord!

Collect

Most gracious and merciful God, in Christ You made it possible for our sins to be washed away so that we might come before You with humble and grateful hearts. We give You our love and praise. In Christ we pray. Amen.

Prayer Of Confession

Lord, we have allowed ourselves to forget that it is only through Your mercy and grace that we are declared righteous in Your sight. We even allow ourselves to think we might be worthy of Your salvation but we are quick to judge others as if You had called us to do so. Forgive us, Lord, and keep us aware that we are saved only by Your grace. In Christ we pray. Amen.

Hymns

"To God Be The Glory"
"I Know Whom I Have Believed"
"O Master, Let Me Walk With Thee"

Fifth Sunday After Epiphany

First Lesson: Isaiah 6:1-8 (9-13)
Theme: Send me, Lord!

Call To Worship

Leader: Let all who would serve the risen Christ gather this day for worship!

People: We would serve the Lord with all our hearts, our souls and our minds.

Leader: Will we be true to the Lord even if the world would reject us?

People: With God's help we will be faithful as witnesses to the world of Christ.

Leader: Then let us praise the Lord and seek God's service which we are to be about.

All: Blessed be the name of the Lord!

Collect

O God, since the days of the ancient ones You have called us only to be faithful and to serve You and You promised to make us a blessing into the world. Use us again, Lord, to be blessings. In Christ we pray. Amen.

Prayer Of Confession

Lord, so often we have not been like Isaiah, but instead we have allowed ourselves to be distracted by the world around us. Too often we have allowed the noises of our culture to keep us from hearing Your call. Forgive us, Lord, and once again restore us to be ready to serve You and witness for You in the world around us today. In Christ we pray. Amen.

Hymns

"Send Your Word"
"Make Me A Blessing"
"Send Me"

Fifth Sunday After Epiphany

Second Lesson: 1 Corinthians 15:1-11
Theme: Share the Good News

Call To Worship

Leader: Let us proclaim the Word of the Lord for all the world to hear!

People: We are witnesses by grace to God's redeeming love for all to see.

Leader: Even while we were yet in sin Christ died for our salvation.

People: Then let us not be slow to share the Good News of God's love.

Leader: Let the joy of our salvation be heard in our songs and our praise.

All: Blessed be the name of the Lord!

Collect

Most gracious and merciful God, in Your loving wisdom You opened the way for our salvation even while we were yet sinful. Give us the strength to lead others to receive Your love. In Christ we pray. Amen.

Prayer Of Confession

Lord, so often we have taken for granted the salvation You have provided for us through Your loving grace. Too often we have seen it only as a gift meant to be received and treasured but not to be passed on as a blessing to others. Forgive us, Lord, and quicken our spirits once again that our joy might shine forth and be a blessing to the lost. In Christ we pray. Amen.

Hymns

"Praise Him, Praise Him"
"Rescue The Perishing"
"Jesus Calls Us"

47

Fifth Sunday After Epiphany

Gospel: Luke 5:1-11
Theme: Fishing for the lost

Call To Worship

Leader: Let all who would be servants of the Lord come together this day.

People: But our powers are so limited and our spirits are so weak.

Leader: Let our hearts be focused on the Lord as our guide and our strength,

People: For we give witness to God's glory and not to our works alone.

Leader: And let our praises ring out for the one true Almighty God's love.

All: Blessed be the name of the Lord!

Collect

O Lord, our God, You have called us to fish in all the lands of the world for the lost who need to hear of Your redeeming mercy and grace. Guide us to those who most need to hear of You. In Christ we pray. Amen.

Prayer Of Confession

Lord, we so often depend only on our own wisdom and efforts to do the works of Your Kingdom, and we fail to seek or to follow Your will. Lord, we often close out Your wonderful blessings in the Church and in our personal lives by thinking we must live life on our own. Forgive us, Lord, and help us once again to open our hearts to Your Lordship. In Christ we pray. Amen.

Hymns

"Higher Ground"
"I Am Thine, O Lord"
"Let The Lower Lights Be Burning"

Sixth Sunday After Epiphany

First Lesson: Jeremiah 17:5-10
Theme: Well-placed faith

Call To Worship

Leader: Let the children of God join in this day in praise and song!

People: The Lord is our salvation and we are safe in God's loving care.

Leader: No power on Earth can stand against the power of Almighty God.

People: No danger in the Universe can snatch us from God's loving hand.

Leader: Then let our voices sound forth in song and praise to Almighty God.

All: Blessed be the name of the Lord!

Collect

O Lord, You are indeed the Creator and Sustainer of all the Universe. Give us the courage and strength to place our present and our eternity in Your loving care. We praise You, Lord. In Christ we pray. Amen.

Prayer Of Confession

Lord, so often we allow ourselves to seek our safety and security in the powers and the personalities of the world, and we fail to remember that they are only people but You are truly God. Too often we chase after any other temptation to find security rather than humble ourselves and turn to You who controls our eternity. Forgive us, O Lord. In Christ we pray. Amen.

Hymns

"Standing On The Promises"
"My Hope Is Built On Nothing Less"
"It Is Well With My Soul"

Sixth Sunday After Epiphany

Second Lesson: 1 Corinthians 15:12-20
Theme: Proclaiming the resurrection

Call To Worship

Leader: Let all who worship the risen Christ enter now into God's house!

People: Because Christ is risen the forces of Evil will not prevail.

Leader: The grave will not keep the faithful from their Lord Jesus Christ.

People: Our eternity belongs to the Lord, and Almighty God will be victorious.

Leader: Then let us not be afraid and let us lift our praise to Almighty God.

All: Blessed be the name of the Lord!

Collect

O God, in Your most loving way You gave us the resurrection of Christ so we might have courage and faith that our eternity truly is in Your hands. Help us to proclaim Your Good News, Lord. In Christ we pray. Amen.

Prayer Of Confession

Lord, we have allowed ourselves to think only in the present, and we have not considered the future, much less eternity. We have often made our decisions in life based not on Your will for us, but on our personal wants in life. Forgive us, Lord, and help us view life as You have called us to see it, so that we might move beyond ourselves to eternity. In Christ we pray. Amen.

Hymns

"He Lives"
"He Touched Me"
"I Need Thee Every Hour"

Sixth Sunday After Epiphany

Gospel: Luke 6:17-26
Theme: Who are the blessed?

Call To Worship

Leader: Let all who have known the blessings of God come together!

People: But our hearts yearn for the Lord and the world does not accept us.

Leader: Blessed are all who hunger and are rejected for the sake of the Lord.

People: Our hearts are saddened by all who reject and scorn God's love.

Leader: Our sadness reflects the very love of God Jesus came to bring us.

All: Blessed be the name of the Lord!

Collect

Almighty and merciful God, in Your infinite wisdom You have claimed those rejected by the world to be among Your beloved ones. Help us to love others as You do, Lord. In Christ we pray. Amen.

Prayer Of Confession

Lord, so often we have accepted the ways of the world and lost sight of the witness You would have our lives be. We choose safety and comfort rather than stand boldly and proclaim Your mercy and grace. Too often we seek the world's acceptance and do not risk rejection by proclaiming Your love. Forgive us, Lord. In Christ we pray. Amen.

Hymns

"I Heard An Old, Old Story"
"God Of Grace And God Of Glory"
"Rescue The Perishing"

Seventh Sunday After Epiphany

First Lesson: Genesis 45:3-11, 15
Theme: God's promise fulfilled

Call To Worship

Leader: The Lord is faithful and God's Word will never return empty!

People: We are sealed before God through the cross and the Word of our Lord.

Leader: All who will seek the Lord in their lives will find God's Word faithful.

People: Each one who has humbly come to the Lord has found God's mercy and grace.

Leader: Let our songs and praise be lifted high for all to hear of God's Word.

All: Blessed be the name of the Lord!

Collect

O Lord, our Savior and our God, only You can be trusted to be just and true in all matters of life itself. Help us to hear Your Word afresh today and live our lives on its foundation. In Christ we pray. Amen.

Prayer Of Confession

Lord, sometimes amid the stresses and strains of everyday life we have become fearful and anxious because we have forgotten Your Word and we have sought to depend too much on our own resources. Forgive us, Lord, and restore in us the passion and vitality Your presence in our lives brings so others, too, may come to know Your Word is true. In Christ we pray. Amen.

Hymns

"How Firm A Foundation"
"Love Lifted Me"
"More Love To Thee, O Christ"

Seventh Sunday After Epiphany

Second Lesson: 1 Corinthians 15:35-38, 42-50
Theme: We shall be raised to eternity

Call To Worship

Leader: Let us celebrate the grace and mercy of our Lord Jesus Christ!

People: We give praise to the Lord for our salvation to eternal life.

Leader: And let us share the Good News for the lost of the world to hear.

People: Yes, we were lost, yet the Lord sent us witness of salvation in Christ.

Leader: Then let us proclaim the love of God through all the streets and nations.

All: Blessed be the name of the Lord!

Collect

Almighty and most loving God, through Your mercy and grace You sent the Christ so that our sins might be forgiven and we might have eternal life. O Lord, we give You our love and praise. In Christ we pray. Amen.

Prayer Of Confession

Lord, we have so often failed to comprehend the wonderful gift of eternal life You have made possible to all who will believe and live their faith. We have too often lived our lives with only a vision for the moment or the day, but seldom have we remembered that You have promised us eternity. Forgive us, Lord, and help us live our faith for all to see. In Christ we pray. Amen.

Hymns

"More Like The Master"
"Near To The Heart Of God"
"Living For Jesus"

Seventh Sunday After Epiphany

Gospel: Luke 6:27-38
Theme: Judge not!

Call To Worship

Leader: Let all who would know the loving ways of the Lord come together.

People: But our lives are so flawed and we are so marked by our ways of sin.

Leader: The Lord's grace is real; we enter today forgiven of all our sins.

People: What does God ask of us as we come together to worship this day?

Leader: That we freely forgive all others as we ourselves have been forgiven.

All: Blessed be the name of the Lord!

Collect

Almighty and most merciful God, through Your love and grace you sent the Christ as our example for living and as our promise that we might have eternal life. O Lord, we give You our lives and our praise. In Christ we pray. Amen.

Prayer Of Confession

Lord, so often forgiveness has been hard for us to accept. You freely gave us Your grace and Your mercy, yet we have been slow and begrudged letting go of our anger and resentments. Too often, Lord, we have failed to forgive others or to pass on the forgiving love You first gave to us. Forgive us, Lord, and soften our hearts, that we may love others. In Christ we pray. Amen.

Hymns

"Love, Mercy, And Grace"
"Jesus, Lover Of My Soul"
"Amazing Grace"

Eighth Sunday After Epiphany

First Lesson: Isaiah 55:10-13
Theme: The Word of the Lord shall bear witness

Call To Worship

Leader: Let us praise God and share the Gospel of Christ in every land!

People: But how will people know our witness is true and genuine?

Leader: The Word of the Lord will speak through our lives and words.

People: Just as we heard the Good News, we are called to share it with others.

Leader: Then let us share it freely and openly and let our joy resound.

All: Blessed be the name of the Lord!

Collect

O Lord, our most wonderful Savior, in Your gracious love You have granted to us Your salvation, not for us to keep, but for us to share with all around us. Give us the vision to keep sharing it. In Christ we pray. Amen.

Prayer Of Confession

O God, You heard our cries and prepared for us a plan of salvation, calling us to be Your witnesses in the world today. Too often, Lord, we have received Your grace and mercy, but we have not been willing to share it as You commanded us. Forgive us, Lord, and give us the courage and strength to share Your Gospel wherever we go all the days of our lives. In Christ we pray. Amen.

Hymns

"All Glory, Laud, And Honor"
"O Love Divine, What Hast Thou Done"
"There Is A Fountain Filled With Blood"

Eighth Sunday After Epiphany

Second Lesson: 1 Corinthians 15:51-58
Theme: Hear God's wonderful mystery

Call To Worship

Leader: Come, hear the wonderful mystery of our Lord and Savior Jesus Christ!

People: For Jesus came, God with us, and set aside all glory for our sake.

Leader: Then Jesus died on the cross, at the hands of mortals, to give us life.

People: Yet God's victory over death is clear in the resurrection of Christ.

Leader: These things we cannot explain, yet each proclaims the glory of God!

All: Blessed be the name of the Lord!

Collect

Most loving and wonderful God, in Your divine wisdom which surpasses our mortal ability to fully comprehend, You sent the Christ to redeem and restore us. We praise You, Lord. In Christ we pray. Amen.

Prayer Of Confession

O God, we have been quick to rely only on our wisdom and science to understand life, and we have too quickly dismissed the wonderful mysteries of our faith. If we cannot explain a matter, we deny it has any truth within it. Forgive us, Lord, and help us celebrate that the Gospel of Christ goes beyond the limitations of our mere mortal minds. In Christ we pray. Amen.

Hymns

"Wonderful Words Of Life"
"Tell Me The Story Of Jesus"
"When I Survey The Wondrous Cross"

Eighth Sunday After Epiphany

Gospel: Luke 6:39-49
Theme: Following the wisdom of Christ

Call To Worship

Leader: Let us come together to focus our thoughts upon the Lord!

People: Let us set aside all that would take our eyes away from God.

Leader: Lord, give us wisdom that we may know Your ways from our own;

People: And bring us together in the unity only Your Holy Spirit brings.

Leader: In the blessed harmony of God's love, give praise unto the Lord!

All: Blessed be the name of the Lord!

Collect

Almighty Creator God, Your ways are not our ways, but You have called us to follow You and learn to love one another. Guide us, O Lord, into Your wonderful paths of righteousness. In Christ we pray. Amen.

Prayer Of Confession

Lord, so often we argue about the small things or are divided over what we see as major issues of the faith, and we do not hear Your commandment to "love one another." We give witness to division and strife rather than Your unity and harmony. Help us today, Lord, to share Your presence and love with all we meet around us. In Christ we pray. Amen.

Hymns

"In Christ There Is No East Or West"
"Lift High The Cross Of Jesus"
"What A Friend We Have In Jesus"

Transfiguration Of Our Lord

First Lesson: Exodus 34:29-35
Theme: God's presence among us

Call To Worship

Leader: Let all who know the wonderful joy of God's love come now for worship!

People: The mercy and grace of the Lord draw us ever closer in Christ.

Leader: The Lord is our redeemer and our guide and is with us in all we do.

People: It is the Lord who is our strength and our courage in adversity.

Leader: Then let us give praise to the Lord, who is present with us even now.

All: Blessed be the name of the Lord!

Collect

O Lord God of Hosts, only You are able to be with us wherever we go or whatever the circumstances. Lead us every hour, O Lord, just as You led Moses and Your children out of Egypt. In Christ we pray. Amen.

Prayer Of Confession

Lord, we have often been like spoiled children, demanding more and more even while we grow less and less willing to submit to Your Lordship in every part of our lives. Forgive us, Lord, and call us again to follow You. Give us the wisdom, strength, and courage to reach out in faith to trust You absolutely no matter what the world would teach us. In Christ we pray. Amen.

Hymns

"Jesus, United By Thy Grace"
"Jesus, Lord, We Look To Thee"
"More Love To Thee, O Christ"

Transfiguration Of Our Lord

Second Lesson: 2 Corinthians 3:12—4:2
Theme: The glory of the Lord shines in us

Call To Worship
Leader: Come, let the light of God's love shine through us now as we worship!

People: We carry the light of Christ into all the nations of the world.

Leader: And we carry the light of Christ into our everyday lives as well.

People: For we are the living witnesses that God's forgiveness and love are real.

Leader: Then let us sing and give praise for our redemption and salvation.

All: Blessed be the name of the Lord!

Collect
O God, in Your righteousness You could have demanded that we face the consequences of our sins, yet You chose to redeem us so we might become Your light in the world. We praise You, Lord. In Christ we pray. Amen.

Prayer Of Confession
O Lord, sometimes we have used the light You have given us only for our own purposes instead of trying to lead others out of their darkness to You. Too often, Lord, we have even tried to snuff out our light so we would not be responsible before You. Forgive us, Lord, and restore within us the light of Your love so we might end darkness all over the world. In Christ we pray. Amen.

Hymns
"There's Within My Heart A Melody"
"Make Me A Blessing"
"Here I Am, Lord"

59

Transfiguration Of The Lord

Gospel: Luke 9:28-36 (37-43)
Theme: Taking the mountaintops into the world

Call To Worship

Leader: Let all who would seek the ways of the Lord come together.

People: We each one seek the mountaintop experiences God has for our lives.

Leader: But are we willing to return to the valley to share God's love?

People: Yes, we will build a fine temple on the highest mountain for the Lord.

Leader: Truly I tell you, the temple of Christ is found only in our hearts.

All: Blessed be the name of the Lord!

Collect

O God, in Your righteousness You could have demanded that we face the consequences of our sins, yet You chose to redeem us so we might become Your light in the world. We praise You, Lord. In Christ we pray. Amen.

Prayer Of Confession

Lord, so often You have touched our lives in loving and healing ways, only to have us turn away from Your call to share Your love with the world. So many times You have heard our cries and led us out of the wilderness, only to see us chase after other worldly pursuits. Forgive us, Lord, and help us focus on our mission as Your Church today. In Christ we pray. Amen.

Hymns

"I Love Thy Kingdom, Lord"
"Christ, Upon The Mountain Peak"
"Christ, Whose Glory Fills The Skies"

Ash Wednesday

First Lesson: Joel 2:1-2, 12-17
Theme: Repent and turn to the Lord

Call To Worship

Leader: Let all who have received God's mercy come in repentance this day.
People: For even as we have been forgiven we have sinned before the Lord.
Leader: God calls to the faithful to repent and come before the Cross.
People: For at the Cross we are again washed clean.
Leader: And at the Cross we were called into the family of Almighty God!
All: Blessed be the name of the Lord!

Collect

O God, even though we are sinners, in Your mercy You have called us to repent and become members in Christ of Your family. Lead us, O Lord, back into Your ways. In Christ we pray. Amen.

Prayer Of Confession

Lord, in the passing of the days we have each again fallen short of the glory and blessings You intended our lives to be. Forgive us, Lord, and help us to return our focus to the cross and to turn our ways back to Your ways that we might bring honor and blessings to Your Holy Name. Through Christ our blessed Lord and Redeemer we lift our prayers. Amen.

Hymns

"Blessed Assurance"
"Yield Not Temptation"
"I Need Thee Every Hour"

Ash Wednesday

Second Lesson: 2 Corinthians 5:20b—6:10
Theme: Faithful servants unto the Lord

Call To Worship

Leader: Let us come together, all who are brothers and sisters in Christ.

People: For Christ died that we might have eternal salvation.

Leader: Then let us live in the ways the Lord taught us to live.

People: And let us set our hearts to choose the ways of Christ each day.

Leader: For the true followers of Christ Judgment Day will bring glory.

All: Blessed be the name of the Lord!

Collect

O God, through the prophets You called the nations to repent. Through Christ You call us each one to repent and turn to follow Your will. Lord, sustain us and lead us home to You. In Christ we pray. Amen.

Prayer Of Confession

Lord, so often in the everyday matters of living we have allowed ourselves to slip little by little and day by day away from the paths You have called us to walk. Forgive us, God, and open our spiritual eyes that we might again see where we have fallen short, and help us to recommit all that we are to being the best servants we can be. In Christ our Lord we pray. Amen.

Hymns

"Rescue The Perishing"
"O Master, Let Me Walk With Thee"
"Take My Life And Let It Be"

Ash Wednesday

Gospel: Matthew 6:1-6, 16-21
Theme: Personal repentance

Call To Worship

Leader: Come, let all who would follow Christ gather this day and repent.

People: Let us weigh the goals in our lives and know our innermost hearts.

Leader: The Lord has called us to be true and in all things to be faithful.

People: Then let us set our hearts upon the ways of the Lord.

Leader: And let our hearts be filled with joy for God's redeeming grace.

All: Blessed be the name of the Lord!

Collect

O God, in Your love and wisdom You have called us to repentance not for punishment but that we should know eternal joy. By Your strong and gentle hand, Lord, lead us back to Your fold. In Christ we pray. Amen.

Prayer Of Confession

Lord, You have called each of us to be faithful and in Your mercy and grace granted us each Your eternal life. But we have each fallen and failed You, and we have each chosen to go our own ways. Forgive us, Lord, and once again open our hearts to Your divine guidance that You might draw us back to Your loving care. In Christ we pray. Amen.

Hymns

"He Leadeth Me"
"Pass Me Not"
"Just As I Am"

First Sunday In Lent

First Lesson: Deuteronomy 26:1-11
Theme: Do we remember the Lord?

Call To Worship

Leader: Let all who know the wonder of the Lord gather now for worship!

People: The Lord is our strength and our salvation all the days of our lives.

Leader: The Lord has redeemed us so all might know of God's loving grace.

People: Let us remember we are redeemed by the blood of our Lord Jesus Christ.

Leader: Let us be faithful to the Lord and lift our voices to share God's love.

All: Blessed be the name of the Lord!

Collect

O God, we are so grateful that You have opened the door for us to be a part of your kingdom. Help us, Lord, to see more clearly every day those things You call us to do. In Christ we pray. Amen.

Prayer Of Confession

Lord, we have often taken for granted the wonderful ways we have experienced Your mercy and grace. We have even taken far too lightly the price You paid so that we might know Your salvation. Forgive us, Lord, and help us always to remember Your call on our lives and that only You are our hope and our Redeemer. In Christ we pray. Amen.

Hymns

"O Thou, In Whose Presence"
"Stand By Me"
"The Old Rugged Cross"

First Sunday In Lent

Second Lesson: Romans 10:8b-13
Theme: Call upon the name of the Lord

Call To Worship

Leader: Call upon the name of the Lord, for only in Christ are we saved!

People: We have known the mercy of God and we have truly received God's grace.

Leader: Then let us proclaim the wonder of God's love to all who will hear.

People: And let us lead all we meet to call upon the Lord for their salvation.

Leader: Together we are the family of the living God, Creator of the Universe.

All: Blessed be the name of the Lord!

Collect

O God, we are so grateful You have called us to be a part of Your kingdom and ministry in our world today. Soften our hearts, Lord, that You might freely use us. In Christ we pray. Amen.

Prayer Of Confession

Lord, we have so often allowed ourselves to seek after every temptation the world has been able to place before us instead of calling only on You. We have sought after wealth, youth, power, and even other religions, for in them we thought we would find life. We have been slow to turn to You. Forgive us, Lord, and receive us again as Your children. In Christ we pray. Amen.

Hymns

"We Praise Thee, O God"
"He Keeps Me Singing"
"I Need Thee Every Hour"

First Sunday In Lent

Gospel: Luke 4:1-13
Theme: Temptation of Jesus

Call To Worship

Leader: Let all who have known temptations and trials come together this day.

People: The temptations of life are too hard and the trials are too long.

Leader: Take courage and let us seek the Lord's strength to sustain us.

People: The Tempter's call would lead us away from the Lord into darkness.

Leader: But the Lord has defeated the evil one and in Christ is our victory.

All: Blessed be the name of the Lord!

Collect

Most gracious and merciful God, even in our times of greatest temptation You have promised You will stand with us and be our strength if we will only turn to You. We praise You, O Lord. In Christ we pray. Amen.

Prayer Of Confession

Lord, we have often let the lure of the world's ways draw us away from the standard of faith and love You taught us to live by. Instead of standing boldly as witnesses of Your mercy and truth, we have bowed in the wind as we sought the world's approval and glory. Forgive us, Lord, and give us the courage to stand true. In Christ we pray. Amen.

Hymns

"O God, Our Help In Ages Past"
"Rock Of Ages"
"Give Me Thine Heart"

Second Sunday In Lent

First Lesson: Genesis 15:1-12, 17-18
Theme: Faith in God's covenant

Call To Worship

Leader: Come, let all who trust in God's New Covenant gather now for worship!

People: For the Lord is faithful and true and God's word will endure forever.

Leader: Neither life nor death nor even the passage of time reduces God's love.

People: Even when all else might fail us the Lord's word will be our solid rock.

Leader: Then let us celebrate and give praise for God's word forever.

All: Blessed be the name of the Lord!

Collect

O God, in Your infinite wisdom You gave us Your New Covenant even when You knew we were yet sinners in need of Your mercy and grace. In every way, Lord, continue to call us ever closer to You. In Christ we pray. Amen.

Prayer Of Confession

Lord, as we have been faced with the storms of life we have often forgotten the New Covenant You gave us, and we have turned instead to our own wisdom for our strength and comfort. Too often, Lord, our faith has not been in You but only in what we can see and understand. Forgive us, Lord, and restore our souls that we might be living witnesses to Your love today. In Christ we pray. Amen.

Hymns

"My Hope Is Built On Nothing Less"
"How Firm A Foundation"
"His Way With Thee"

Second Sunday In Lent

Second Lesson: Philippians 3:17—4:1
Theme: Stand firm in Christ

Call To Worship

Leader: Let all who would call upon the Lord gather now for worship!

People: The Lord is our salvation and our rock against the storms of life.

Leader: The Lord has walked beside us all the days of our lives.

People: And we are called to proclaim God's wonderful blessings for all to hear.

Leader: Then let us lift our voices together in praise and song before our God.

All: Blessed be the name of the Lord!

Collect

Almighty and loving God, You have so wonderfully blessed us with Your salvation and charged us with sharing it with all who will hear us. Give us the courage, Lord, to share Your Gospel. In Christ we pray. Amen.

Prayer Of Confession

Lord, so many times when we have had the chance to share the wonderful news of what You have done in our lives we have been silent. Too often, Lord, we have even chosen to call our salvation too personal to share. Forgive us, O God, and fill us again with the excitement of Your love so we might bubble forth for all to hear of Your loving mercy and grace. In Christ we pray. Amen.

Hymns

"Stand Up, Stand Up For Jesus"
"Blessed Assurance"
"I Surrender All"

Second Sunday In Lent

Gospel: Luke 13:31-35
Theme: Fear not the threats of the world

Call To Worship

Leader: Let us come together in the name of our Lord Jesus Christ!

People: But there is so much in the world we fear, so much that threatens us.

Leader: Why should we fear the world when we are safely held in God's hands?

People: But there are so many with power who lay claim upon our very lives.

Leader: Yet it is the Lord God Almighty alone who holds our eternity.

All: Blessed be the name of the Lord!

Collect

Almighty God, Creator of the Universe, You have called us to be Your obedient servants in the face of whatever may come, and You have promised eternity will be ours. Give us Your strength, Lord. In Christ we pray. Amen.

Prayer Of Confession

Lord, so often we have allowed the people and things of the world to control our lives instead of You. We have sought the approval of others and taken You for granted. We have chased after the things of the world that are only temporary and ignored You and eternity. Forgive us, Lord, and give us the courage and vision to be faithful. In Christ we pray. Amen.

Hymns

"True Hearted, Whole Hearted"
"O Jesus, I Have Promised"
"More Like The Master"

Third Sunday In Lent

First Lesson: Isaiah 55:1-9
Theme: Seek ye first the Lord

Call To Worship

Leader: Let all who seek the will of the Lord enter God's house for worship!

People: Only in serving the Lord will we find true meaning and joy in life.

Leader: The Lord alone is our sustainer and defender no matter what may come.

People: Then let us seek the will of the Lord in every path of our lives.

Leader: Let joyous praise and song abound as we worship the Lord our God!

All: Blessed be the name of the Lord!

Collect

Almighty and merciful God, in Your loving way You have called us each to be Your obedient servants no matter what the demands of this world might be. Help us to follow only You, Lord. In Christ we pray. Amen.

Prayer Of Confession

Lord, so often the honors and rewards the world has to offer have been more important to us than seeking Your will for our lives. Too often, we have sought only to satisfy our own desires and wants and have turned away from the call You would place on our lives. Forgive us, Lord, and give us the strength and courage to be Your obedient servants. In Christ we pray. Amen.

Hymns

"I Am Thine, O Lord"
"To God Be The Glory"
"O Master, Let Me Walk With Thee"

Third Sunday In Lent

Second Lesson: 1 Corinthians 10:1-13
Theme: Remembering who we are

Call To Worship

Leader: Let all who worship the Lord God Almighty gather now for worship!

People: For we are a part of God's family called to share the Gospel today.

Leader: And we are to take God's light of truth into all of the world.

People: We are the witnesses that the Good News of Christ is true today.

Leader: Then let us proclaim the Gospel of Christ in word and joyful song.

All: Blessed be the name of the Lord!

Collect

O God, in Your eternal wisdom You call us to be no less than Your beloved children, not so we can gloat but so we may share Your wonderful love with others. Help us reach others for You, Lord. In Christ we pray. Amen.

Prayer Of Confession

O God, we often show that we have forgotten we are a part of Your family when we fail to love others as You have called us to love. Sometimes we act puffed up and pompous as if we were actually worthy to be called by Your name. Forgive us, Lord, and help us to remember that it is only by Your mercy and grace that we have righteousness, and we are to share Christ with the world. In Christ we pray. Amen.

Hymns

"Come, We That Love The Lord"
"We've A Story To Tell To The Nations"
"Beneath The Cross Of Jesus"

Third Sunday In Lent

Gospel: Luke 13:1-9
Theme: The lesson of the fig tree

Call To Worship

Leader: Come, let our hearts be turned with praise toward the Lord.

People: But the cares and concerns of life have drawn us away from the Lord.

Leader: The Lord our God is merciful and with love calls us to return home.

People: But we have fallen so short of all that God would have us to be.

Leader: Yet through the grace of our Lord Jesus Christ we are welcomed home.

All: Blessed be the name of the Lord!

Collect

Almighty God, Creator of all the Universe, in Your divine mercy and grace You have given us this season to bring forth fruit for Your kingdom. Cultivate us, Lord, and help us to produce good fruit. In Christ we pray. Amen.

Prayer Of Confession

Lord, so often we have strayed away from being the living witnesses of Your love that You intended us to be. Too often the stresses and strains of life have challenged our faith and lead us away from our commitment to serve in whatever way You would use us. Forgive us, Lord, and give us the courage to return to Your loving care and guidance. In Christ we pray. Amen.

Hymns

"Give Your Best To The Master"
"Make Me A Blessing"
"I'll Go Where You Want Me To Go"

Fourth Sunday In Lent

First Lesson: Joshua 5:9-12
Theme: With God's help we can!

Call To Worship

Leader: Let us gather together this day and celebrate the blessings of God!

People: With God's help we can face the problems and dangers of tomorrow.

Leader: Who indeed can stand against the power and might of the Lord our God?

People: No force in all creation can endure against God or without God's help.

Leader: Praise be to God who has sustained us all the days of our lives.

All: Blessed be the name of the Lord!

Collect

O God, even in the days of Moses Your mercy and grace sustained us and carried us through the worst of times. Lord, give us the courage and faith to trust You as Moses did. In Christ we pray. Amen.

Prayer Of Confession

Lord, we have often been reluctant to enter into Your ministries for fear we did not have the resources or the strength to do the task. Too often we have seen only what was available for use in ministry in the world around us, and we have forgotten about the manna You can provide. Forgive us, Lord, and call us again to trust You and to serve others. In Christ we pray. Amen.

Hymns

"Come, We That Love The Lord"
"Come, Christians, Join To Sing"
"Others"

Fourth Sunday In Lent

Second Lesson: 2 Corinthians 5:16-21
Theme: Being ambassadors for Christ

Call To Worship

Leader: Let us each proclaim the glory of the Lord for all the world to hear!

People: God has been so gracious unto us and blessed us in so many ways.

Leader: Blessings are meant to be shared and God's wonder should be known by all.

People: Then let our voices be raised to proclaim God's wonder and majesty.

Leader: And let our hearts be filled with joyful praise for our loving God.

All: Blessed be the name of the Lord!

Collect

Most loving and merciful God, in Your divine plan You have adopted us and blessed us with Your presence so that the whole world might hear of Your love. Help us share the Good News, Lord. In Christ we pray. Amen.

Prayer Of Confession

Lord, You have been so gracious unto us, yet so often we have expected even more from You. You have called us to share the joy of being in Your kingdom, yet too often we have remained silent or we have allowed ourselves to feel that we truly deserve Your blessings. Forgive us, Lord, and renew our spirits so that we may tell others of Your love. In Christ we pray. Amen.

Hymns

"There's Within My Heart A Melody"
"He Lifted Me"
"I'll Go Where You Want Me To Go"

Fourth Sunday In Lent

Gospel: Luke 15:1-3, 11b-32
Theme: Wayward children

Call To Worship

Leader: Let us come together as part of God's beloved family.

People: We are indeed God's children. Let us gather today in God's house.

Leader: We have been faithful at times and we have strayed at times from God's love.

People: But God has never given up on us, always awaiting our return home.

Leader: God's love for us is so real that Jesus came to lead the lost home.

All: Blessed be the name of the Lord!

Collect

O God, like a loving parent You have always watched over us, even when we were intent on running away from You. We thank You, Lord, and we give You our heartfelt love. In Christ we pray. Amen.

Prayer Of Confession

Lord, so many times we have wandered off in our own directions, chasing after our dreams, only to wake up and find ourselves completely lost without You. We have focused only on the present and forgotten You are the God of Eternity. We have failed You, yet You love us still. Forgive us, Lord, and lead us lovingly home. In Christ we pray. Amen.

Hymns

"Come, Sinners, To The Gospel Feast"
"I Stand Amazed In The Presence"
"O Jesus, I Have Promised"

Fifth Sunday In Lent

First Lesson: Isaiah 43:16-21
Theme: To God alone belongs the glory

Call To Worship

Leader: Come, let all of God's people give praise and worship the Lord!

People: For we are the handiwork of the Lord God Almighty.

Leader: The Lord has called us to repentance and has forgiven our sins in Christ.

People: We are not yet perfect, but God is molding and working with us always.

Leader: Then let us give our hearts, filled with loving praise, to the Lord daily.

All: Blessed be the name of the Lord!

Collect

O Lord, You are indeed the Potter and we are Your clay. Mold and shape us, O God, into the people You would have us to be in the image of Christ. And help us proclaim Your glory, Lord. In Christ we pray. Amen.

Prayer Of Confession

Lord, so often when You have blessed us within full view of the seeking world around us, we have taken credit for Your works as if we had done them all on our own. Too often, Lord, we have failed to make any mention of giving the glory and credit to You. Forgive us, Lord, and help us to be quick to give You the praise and glory for all the world to see. In Christ we pray. Amen.

Hymns

"To God Be The Glory"
"Love Divine"
"I Need Thee Every Hour"

Fifth Sunday In Lent

Second Lesson: Philippians 3:4b-14
Theme: Ever onward in Christ

Call To Worship

Leader: Let us seek the will of the Lord in each and every day of our lives!

People: For the Lord is our Good Shepherd and we need not fear tomorrow.

Leader: God is faithful and true and we can celebrate best by trusting the Lord.

People: No other is so wonderful and wise. There is none to compare with God.

Leader: Let our hearts and voices be joined as we sing and give praise to God.

All: Blessed be the name of the Lord!

Collect

Almighty and merciful God, You have lovingly blessed us and given us Your Word that we should move joyfully into each new day, sharing the Gospel of Christ as we go. We praise You, Lord. In Christ we pray. Amen.

Prayer Of Confession

Lord, You have blessed us and given us the Holy Spirit so that we should not walk alone in this world, yet so often we are cowed by our fears and thoughts of tomorrow. Forgive us, Lord, and touch us again so that we might draw from Your presence in our hearts the assurance we need to challenge the world for You and no longer be slowed or stopped by our fears. In Christ we pray. Amen.

Hymns

"O God, Our Help In Ages Past"
"Blessed Assurance"
"Holy Spirit, Faithful Guide"

Fifth Sunday In Lent

Gospel: John 12:1-8
Theme: Worship from the heart

Call To Worship

Leader: Come, let us gather together this day and worship the Lord!

People: Let us lift our praise to God in our songs and our anthems!

Leader: Let us praise the Lord in our words and our readings,

People: And let us turn our hearts to the Lord whose love has made us whole.

Leader: God's love is so real that Jesus would even suffer the cross for us.

All: Blessed be the name of the Lord!

Collect

O God, Creator and Sustainer of all the universe, in Your infinite mercy You have chosen to call us, who are even yet sinners, into Your loving family. Help us repent and serve You with love. In Christ we pray. Amen.

Prayer Of Confession

Lord, so often we seem to let the demands of life be more important than spending personal time in prayer and worship. Always there are tasks to be done, errands to be about, even the busy pace that caring for others can demand; yet somehow time with You gets forgotten. Forgive us, Lord, and hear our hearts as we seek Your love. In Christ we pray. Amen.

Hymns

"All Creatures Of Our God And King"
"Immortal, Invisible, God Only Wise"
"Near To The Heart Of God"

Palm Sunday
(Sixth Sunday In Lent)

First Lesson: Isaiah 50:4-9a
Theme: We shall not be ashamed

Call To Worship

Leader: Let our voices be raised in praise for our Lord and Savior, Jesus Christ!

People: But many in the world do not want to hear of Jesus or the cross.

Leader: The Word of the Lord will never be defeated nor will it return empty.

People: But we may lose all we hold dear if the world turns against us.

Leader: Only the Lord holds our eternity and the Word of God will not suffer loss!

All: Blessed be the name of the Lord!

Collect

Most gracious and merciful God, You sent us the Christ who died that we might have life, and You call us to share freely Your message of love with all who will hear. Give us Your strength, Lord. In Christ we pray. Amen.

Prayer Of Confession

Lord, so often we have taken for granted the wonderful mission You gave each one of us as we became a part of Your Church. Too often our days have returned to the mundane and we have lost sight of our commission to take Your Light into the darkness wherever we find it. Forgive us, Lord, and restore our passion to serve and live for You. In Christ we pray. Amen.

Hymns

"Are Ye Able?"
"Tell Me The Story Of Jesus"
"When I Survey The Wondrous Cross"

79

Palm Sunday
(Sixth Sunday In Lent)

Second Lesson: Philippians 2:5-11
Theme: We confess Jesus Christ is Lord!

Call To Worship

Leader: Come, let all who confess the name of Christ gather now for worship!

People: We seek to serve the risen Christ as our Lord and Savior.

Leader: Then let our voices carry the name of Christ throughout the world.

People: And let our lives display the love of Christ in whatever we do or say.

Leader: Christ is indeed Lord, so let our voices be raised in praise and song.

All: Blessed be the name of the Lord!

Collect

O Lord, You alone are worthy of our praise and You alone deserve the loyalty and worship of our hearts. Help us share the Good News of Your salvation wherever we may go for all to hear. In Christ we pray. Amen.

Prayer Of Confession

Lord, as we have walked the path toward the cross through this season of Lent, we have often been slow to deal with those times when we have allowed the temptations of the world to take Your holy place in our lives. Forgive us, Christ, and help us to see in our hearts the things we need to give up and turn over to You so that we might serve You better. In Christ we pray. Amen.

Hymns

"Rejoice, The Lord Is King"
"Stand Up, Stand Up For Jesus"
"Beneath The Cross Of Jesus"

Palm Sunday
(Sixth Sunday In Lent)

Gospel: Luke 19:28-40
Theme: Hosanna, King of kings

Call To Worship

Leader: Children of the Living God, let us gather for worship in God's house!

People: God is our redeemer and our Lord and is worthy to be called King of kings.

Leader: No other power in all of creation is likened to the Lord God Almighty.

People: Yet God so loved each and every one of us that Christ died for our sins.

Leader: Sing God's praise with all your heart, for Christ is God with us.

All: Blessed be the name of the Lord!

Collect

O most Holy God, You could well have called us to account for rejecting Your prophets and for placing Christ on the cross, yet You gave us Your mercy and grace instead. We praise You, Lord. In Christ we pray. Amen.

Prayer Of Confession

O God, even after You have shown us Your loving mercy and grace, we have each turned to our own ways, forgetting the price You paid so that we might know Your forgiveness. Too often, Lord, we have begun our days without a thought to how much You have given so we might have life itself. Forgive us, Lord, and call us again to repentance. In Christ we pray. Amen.

Hymns

"Crown Him With Many Crowns"
"Hail To The Lord's Anointed"
"Have Thine Own Way, Lord"

Passion Sunday
(Sixth Sunday In Lent)

First Lesson: Isaiah 50:4-9a
Theme: Christ died for our sins

Call To Worship

Leader: Come, let us give praise for God's wonderful redeeming love!

People: For even while we were lost in our sins, Jesus died for us.

Leader: We were unrighteous, even the best of us, yet Christ died to wash us clean.

People: We enter this house of worship, praising God for our Lord and Savior,

Leader: And our voices proclaim the glory of the Lord God Almighty.

All: Blessed be the name of the Lord!

Collect

Most loving and merciful God, in Your infinite grace You were willing for Christ to die for our sins so that we might not suffer eternal condemnation. Help us to share Your Good News, Lord. In Christ we pray. Amen.

Prayer Of Confession

O God, even as we have reached the week before Easter, it is still difficult for us to fully understand the price You gave so that we should know Salvation. We have often taken the death of Jesus on the cross so lightly that we have hardly given it a second thought. Forgive us, Lord, and draw us ever closer to accepting the crosses You have for us to bear. In Christ we pray. Amen.

Hymns

"Alas! And Did My Savior Bleed"
"Lead Me To Calvary"
"Must Jesus Bear The Cross Alone"

Passion Sunday
(Sixth Sunday In Lent)

Second Lesson: Philippians 2:5-11
Theme: Christ came for our sake

Call To Worship

Leader: Let our hearts be filled with joy; let our souls give praise to God!

People: For we have received the mercy and grace of God in Christ our Lord.

Leader: Christ died on the cross for all sin, even that we today might be saved.

People: Christ died for our sins even as we rejected the message of God's love.

Leader: Surely God is love itself and truly worthy to be worshiped and praised.

All: Blessed be the name of the Lord!

Collect

Most loving and merciful God, in Your divine plan to redeem us You allowed Christ to go to the cross so we might learn the depth of Your love. Truly You are worthy of our deepest praise. In Christ we pray. Amen.

Prayer Of Confession

O God, the thought of losing one of our children is almost more than we can bear, yet we have often taken the price You paid for us so lightly. Lord, we have treated the cross as if it were just a story, and the pain and heartbreak it represents were not real. Forgive us, Lord, and call us anew to take up our crosses and follow You. In Christ we pray. Amen.

Hymns

"Alas! And Did My Savior Bleed"
"The Old Rugged Cross"
"More Love To Thee"

Passion Sunday
(Sixth Sunday In Lent)

Gospel: Luke 22:14—23:56
Theme: The Crucifixion

Call To Worship

Leader: We come together in the house of the Lord only through God's mercy.

People: For we have all sinned and fallen short before the glory of God.

Leader: Yet through Christ, God does not hold our sins before us.

People: Through Christ we walk in freedom and love to reach out to the world.

Leader: In Christ we take compassion and not God's wrath to the world.

All: Blessed be the name of the Lord!

Collect

Almighty and omnipotent God, You watched as we held a mockery of a trial and then nailed Jesus to the cross. Your love was greater than our sin, and we give You our deepest love and praise. In Christ we pray. Amen.

Prayer Of Confession

Lord, so many times we have chosen to hold on to our guilt and our sins and we have failed to accept Your mercy. We hold on to our feelings of being unworthy and deny the message Christ proclaimed of Your love and Your forgiveness. We focus on our own lives and fail to be witnesses to the world of Your grace instead. Forgive us, Lord. In Christ we pray. Amen.

Hymns

"Go To Dark Gethsemane"
"The Old Rugged Cross"
"Must Jesus Bear The Cross Alone"

Maundy Thursday

First Lesson: Exodus 12:1-4 (5-10) 11-14
Theme: Passover

Call To Worship

Leader: Let us come together and worship, all who have received God's mercy!

People: For we were lost and in bondage, yet the Lord has heard our pleas.

Leader: As in the days of Moses, God spared the children of Israel.

People: For there is no god other than the Almighty God of Israel.

Leader: And God's mercy and grace have spared us all.

All: Blessed be the name of the Lord!

Collect

O God, Almighty God of the Universe, even as You spared the children of Israel in the Passover, You have spared us from Your wrath. Lord, help us to reach out and save others. In Christ we pray. Amen.

Prayer Of Confession

Lord, so often we would think we are worthy of Your mercy and forgiveness, and that somehow we deserve to be spared from Your wrath. Forgive us, Lord, for our blindness, for we are each and every one sinners, yet through Christ You have called us Your own. Forgive us, Lord, for our times of rebellion, and continue to shepherd us home. In Christ we pray. Amen.

Hymns

"Guide Me, O Thou Great Jehovah"
"O Love Divine, What Hast Thou Done"
"When I Survey The Wondrous Cross"

Maundy Thursday

Second Lesson: 1 Corinthians 11:23-26
Theme: The Last Supper

Call To Worship

Leader: Come, let us gather together, all who would commune with the Lord.

People: But are we welcome in God's house as sinners before the Lord?

Leader: Christ died on the cross that all sinners might seek God's holy face.

People: Even we who have fallen so deep in sin, may we be at God's holy table?

Leader: As we repent and seek God's mercy, in Christ we are each washed clean.

All: **Blessed be the name of the Lord!**

Collect

O God, You have steadfastly sought to reach out to us and You have even rescued us when we were in rebellion. We are blessed so by Your presence, Lord; lead us to reach out to others. In Christ we pray. Amen.

Prayer Of Confession

Lord, so often we have been willing to receive Your blessings but we have failed to understand that You meant for us to become blessings in the lives of others. Too often we chose to study and learn the Holy Scriptures, but then would rather not share the Gospel with the hurting world around us. Forgive us, Lord, and lead us to witness for You. In Christ we pray. Amen.

Hymns

"Come And Let Us Sweetly Join"
"Love Divine, All Loves Excelling"
"Let Us Break Bread Together"

Maundy Thursday

Gospel: John 13:1-17, 31b-35
Theme: Christian as servant

Call To Worship

Leader: Let us gather together and worship, all who would serve the risen Lord.

People: No greater love can we share than to reach out and care for others.

Leader: Christ, the Lord, chose to be our servant in all He did.

People: In obedience to God Christ died for us on the cross.

Leader: No one is greater than the Master, so let us be servants unto the world.

All: Blessed be the name of the Lord!

Collect

O God, the Gospel is such a paradox to us: to be great we must be willing to serve. Yet Christ set a living example in washing the feet of the disciples. Make us servants, O Lord. In Christ we pray. Amen.

Prayer Of Confession

Lord, so often we would hear a call to greatness, but we would not hear Your call to become the servants of all. Too often we desire to be important, yet we would not choose to wash the feet of the disciples as You did. Forgive us, Lord, for our pride, and do whatever it takes to lead us to love humbly and desire to serve others for You. In Christ we pray. Amen.

Hymns

"In The Garden"
"What Wondrous Love Is This"
"Open My Eyes"

Good Friday

First Lesson: Isaiah 52:13—53:12
Theme: The suffering servant

Call To Worship

Leader: Come, let us celebrate God's love for us in Christ!
People: Jesus knew our rejection and scourging.
Leader: Yet He bore our sorrows and griefs to the cross.
People: Jesus felt the pain of the nails and the hammer.
Leader: Yet for us Christ would die that we might have eternal life.
All: Blessed be the name of the Lord!

Collect

O God, You gave us such a blessing to bear our sins and sorrows for us upon the cross. Lead us, O God, to be more like Christ and less demanding that things should always be our way. In Christ we pray. Amen.

Prayer Of Confession

Lord, so often we would hear of the mercy and grace You have freely extended to all who will repent and serve You, but we would rather not hear the agony that was Yours upon the cross. So often, God, we would hear of our salvation, but we would rather not hear of the suffering and death as the price You paid for it. Forgive us, Lord, is all we can ask. In Christ we pray. Amen.

Hymns

"Hope Of The World"
"Must Jesus Bear The Cross Alone"
"Lead Me To Calvary"

Good Friday

Second Lesson: Hebrews 10:16-25
Theme: The New Covenant

Call To Worship

Leader: Let all who would serve the risen Christ gather for worship this day.

People: For in Christ God gave us a new covenant, so all may have new life.

Leader: Through the cross Christ has made full the Law forever.

People: Yet we are not without God's Laws nor without the Holy Spirit.

Leader: In Christ God has written the Law of love forever on our hearts.

All: Blessed be the name of the Lord!

Collect

O God, as You saw the volumes of rules we had gathered You sent to us a Savior. In Christ You taught us a new way, that we should love You and love one another. We praise You, Lord. In Christ we pray. Amen.

Prayer Of Confession

Lord, so often we have desired to write rules by which to live, yet it would seem the more we write, the more we need. You taught us, Lord, to love God and to love one another, yet so often we still would rather write our own sets of rules until again we find ourselves in bondage. Forgive us, Lord, and help us first to try living by Your love. In Christ we pray. Amen.

Hymns

"Blest Be The Tie That Binds"
"Pass Me Not, O Gentle Savior"
"In Thee Do I Live"

Good Friday

Gospel: John 18:1—19:42
Theme: The Crucifixion

Call To Worship

Leader: Let all who would call Christ their Savior come together today!

People: For we remember just now the trial and the scourging Jesus suffered.

Leader: And we remember the crowds that mocked Him and said Jesus must die.

People: And we remember the disciples who scattered, and how Jesus died alone.

Leader: We remember also the cross, for on it God paid for our salvation.

All: Blessed be the name of the Lord!

Collect

O God, to watch us nail Jesus on the cross must have caused You so much pain. Jesus came so we might know peace and joy, but we rejected Him. Let us tell the world of Christ today. In Christ we pray. Amen.

Prayer Of Confession

Lord, when we hear the story of the cross, so often we are tempted to think of it happening long ago and having nothing to do with us. Yet, Lord, each time we reject the needy or turn our backs on the hurting world around us in favor of our own comfort, we are again rejecting You. Forgive us, Lord; help us to love and care for others. In Christ we pray. Amen.

Hymns

"Alas! And Did My Savior Bleed"
"When I Survey The Wondrous Cross"
"The Way Of The Cross"

Easter

First Lesson: Acts 10:34-43
Theme: Resurrection of the Lord

Call To Worship

Leader: Christ, our Lord, is risen from the dead. Praise be to the Lord!

People: Let us sing songs of great joy and let all hear the good news!

Leader: Christ who died on the Cross is risen on the third day!

People: Just as the prophets foretold, may God's holy name be praised!

Leader: Christ is risen victorious, that all might have eternal life.

All: Blessed be the name of the Lord!

Collect

O God, in the resurrection we became Yours by redemption. Death and the grave no longer can hold Your beloved children. Let us celebrate the good news by sharing it worldwide. In Christ we pray. Amen.

Prayer Of Confession

Lord, so often we have heard the story of the resurrection, yet in our hearts we have doubted it could really be true. So often to find our joy and peace we have tried the ways of the world only to learn none of these really matter. Forgive us, Lord, and today we ask You to take over our lives and lead us again into Your Holy ways. In Christ we pray. Amen.

Hymns

"This Is The Day"
"Easter People, Raise Your Voices"
"The Day Of Resurrection"

Easter

Second Lesson: 1 Corinthians 15:19-26
Theme: Death's bondage broken

Call To Worship

Leader: Praise be to the Lord God Almighty! Jesus Christ lives today!

People: Even though Jesus was nailed to the cross, God is victorious over death!

Leader: No longer can the grave's darkness cause terror for the children of God.

People: No longer can the Evil One hold the children of God in sin's bondage.

Leader: Holy, holy is our God! For Christ came that we may have life eternal!

All: Blessed be the name of the Lord!

Collect

Most loving and merciful God, in Your infinite wisdom You knew the tyranny and bondage death held over us. In the resurrection You set us free. We praise You, O Lord. In Christ we pray. Amen.

Prayer Of Confession

Lord, so often we have lived our lives as if the resurrection had not occurred. We have been timid when You have called us to be bold. We have been silent when You would have had us speak out against hate and injustice. We have been protective of what we have, instead of giving to those in need, as You call us to do. Forgive us, Lord, and renew our faith. In Christ we pray. Amen.

Hymns

"Because He Lives"
"The Old Rugged Cross"
"He Lives"

Easter

Gospel: John 20:1-18
Theme: Resurrection

Call To Worship

Leader: Christ the Lord is risen from the dead! Hallelujah!

People: Sing for joy all ye peoples; the Glory of God has come.

Leader: God's Light truly does shine upon us this day with mercy and love.

People: Unworthy as we are, we are now in the family of God through Christ.

Leader: Give praise to the Lord! God's loving kindness endures forever!

All: Blessed be the name of the Lord!

Collect

O God, in the cross and the resurrection You have paid the price for our eternal redemption. We praise You, O Lord, and ask You to help us carry Your gospel all around the world. In Christ we pray. Amen.

Prayer Of Confession

Lord, through the resurrection of Christ You freed us from the powers of darkness and evil. In Christ, You opened the way for us to enter Your Holy Kingdom. Forgive us when we have failed to walk where You would send us, to love when our loving could have made a difference, or to be Your voice of peace in the world today. In Christ we pray. Amen.

Hymns

"Christ The Lord Is Risen Today"
"Ask Ye What Great Thing I Know"
"The Way Of The Cross Leads Home"

Second Sunday Of Easter

First Lesson: Acts 5:27-32
Theme: We are witnesses sent by God

Call To Worship

Leader: Let us gather this day and raise our voices in praise before God!

People: In God's wonderful mercy we have been given the Lord's salvation.

Leader: Not that we should boast, but that we should proclaim the mercy of God.

People: For it is not our goodness that has made us righteous, but Christ alone.

Leader: Let us call all peoples and nations to the salvation of the risen Christ.

All: Blessed be the name of the Lord!

Collect

Almighty and righteous Lord, You could well have called us into account and held us lacking as we rejected Christ, yet You chose to turn our rejection into Your glory. We give You our praise. In Christ we pray. Amen.

Prayer Of Confession

Lord, so often we have found ourselves in circumstances that would call us to stand firm and give witness of Your mercy and grace, but we were silent. Too often we have even sought to avoid being called upon to witness for You so we might not be openly embarrassed by sharing our faith. Forgive us, Lord, and lead us to those who need to hear of You. In Christ we pray. Amen.

Hymns

"I Love To Tell The Story"
"Pass It On"
"Sent Forth By God's Blessing"

Second Sunday Of Easter

Second Lesson: Revelation 1:4-8
Theme: Priesthood of Christians

Call To Worship

Leader: Let each one enter the house of the Lord this day for worship and praise!

People: Christ has called us to believe and to bear witness to all the world.

Leader: Let our voices be joined in praise and song for God's mercy and grace.

People: And let our hearts be dedicated to telling all we meet about our Lord.

Leader: Let us celebrate our salvation and let us always give God the praise.

All: Blessed be the name of the Lord!

Collect

O God, in Your most loving way You have given us the wonderful gift of salvation and called us to share it with all who will believe. Give us the wisdom and strength to fulfill Your call. In Christ we pray. Amen.

Prayer Of Confession

Lord, sometimes we have acted as if Your priesthood did not rest on our shoulders but was the responsibility of others. Too often we have expected others to keep the faith and spread the Good News when we were the ones You could have used most effectively. Forgive us, Lord, and help us to be more responsible for carrying Your message of love into the world. In Christ we pray. Amen.

Hymns

"O For A Thousand Tongues To Sing"
"Blessed Be The Name"
"I Will Sing The Wondrous Story"

Second Sunday Of Easter

Gospel: John 20:19-31
Theme: Faith beyond doubt

Call To Worship

Leader: There is but one God, Creator of the universe, who loves us all.

People: And all who are led by the Holy Spirit are indeed children of God.

Leader: Come then, and let us walk in the ways of the Lord with gladness!

People: The Holy Spirit is with each one who calls upon the Lord in truth.

Leader: So let us lift our hearts to God in joyful praise and song!

All: Blessed be the name of the Lord!

Collect

O God, You are greater than all we might imagine or even dream, yet in Christ You made Your kingdom open to all who would have faith and believe. Help us to live by faith, Lord. In Christ we pray. Amen.

Prayer Of Confession

Lord, You call to our hearts in the gentle words of peace, and yet so often we will not hear You. In our stressful world You would give love and joy to our lives, yet we fear that Your gifts are too good to be true, so we will not accept them. In love, You offer us life itself, but in our stubborn pride we choose not to receive it. Forgive us, Lord. In Christ we pray. Amen.

Hymns

"Wonderful Words Of Life"
"I Know Whom I Have Believed"
"Let There Be Peace On Earth"

Third Sunday Of Easter

First Lesson: Acts 9:1-6 (7-20)
Theme: Repentance in Christ

Call To Worship

Leader: Give praise to God, for Christ is risen and lives in our hearts!

People: Just as Peter did, we have each denied Christ in our own way.

Leader: But Christ can call us back to the fold, as Paul was called by the Lord.

People: We each must come before Christ and repent of our sins to know salvation.

Leader: In our repentance, let us lift our voices in praise to Almighty God!

All: Blessed be the name of the Lord!

Collect

Almighty God, Creator of the Universe, in the face of hatred and rejection You extend to us peace and love in order that we might repent and know salvation. We thank You and give You our praise. In Christ we pray. Amen.

Prayer Of Confession

Lord, so often when faced with insults we have thought only of anger and revenge, and we have not remembered all the times You were patient and accepting with us. Too often fighting back has been more important than hearing Your Word and being witnesses of Your love in today's world. Forgive us, Lord, and give us Your wisdom to be patient. In Christ we pray. Amen.

Hymns

"Living For Jesus"
"This Is A Day Of New Beginnings"
"Take My Life And Let It Be"

Third Sunday Of Easter

Second Lesson: Revelation 5:11-14
Theme: Come worship the Lord!

Call To Worship

Leader: Let every people of every nation worship the Lord God of Hosts!

People: Let us join the heavenly hosts with our praise for Jesus Christ our Lord.

Leader: For God has decreed that every being will bow down before the Lamb of God.

People: All will one day worship Christ, who suffered that we might have life.

Leader: Then let our hearts be filled with joy and praise before Almighty God!

All: Blessed be the name of the Lord!

Collect

O God, in the Lordship of Christ You have brought us into Your Holy Kingdom, and one day every knee will bow in worship and praise before Christ our eternal King. We praise You, O Lord. In Christ we pray. Amen.

Prayer Of Confession

Lord, sometimes we have let the concerns of the world around us cause us to worry and fret as if You were not really the Lord of all. Too often we have doubted and even forgotten that we are servants of Christ, adopted children of the Lord God Almighty. Forgive us, Lord, and help us remember Your promise to use all things for good in the lives of those who serve You. In Christ we pray. Amen.

Hymns

"Joyful, Joyful, We Adore Thee"
"Crown Him With Many Crowns"
"Spirit Song"

Third Sunday Of Easter

Gospel: John 21:1-19
Theme: Follow Me

Call To Worship

Leader: There is now light where once there was darkness and despair.

People: There is hope and joy where once there was only sadness and shame.

Leader: We have life because Christ lives and the bonds of death are broken.

People: Even as the days grow long and we are weary, the Lord sustains us.

Leader: For Christ alone pleads our case before God so that we may know mercy.

All: Blessed be the name of the Lord!

Collect

Almighty and merciful God, in Your loving way, You ask only for us to have faith and follow You and You promise that we will see wonders we have not imagined. Give us the strength and courage to trust You, Lord. In Christ we pray. Amen.

Prayer Of Confession

Lord, so many times we have chosen to hold on to our sins and deny Your resurrection. We have held on to our feelings of being unworthy and denied the message of forgiveness Christ came to bring us. We have focused on ourselves and failed to be witnesses of Your love to the world. Forgive us, Lord, and make our lives shine for You. In Christ we pray. Amen.

Hymns

"Jesus, Keep Me Near The Cross"
"Spirit Song"
"Others"

Fourth Sunday Of Easter

First Lesson: Acts 9:36-43
Theme: Power over death

Call To Worship

Leader: Our days are limited. Let us use them to serve and praise the Lord!

People: **Yet death is no longer a mystery for those who believe, but a new beginning.**

Leader: We are called to serve the Lord without fear and to be faithful to God.

People: **For the powers of this world, even death, are no match for the Lord.**

Leader: Let us lift our voices in praise for the redeeming love of Christ our Lord.

All: **Blessed be the name of the Lord!**

Collect

Almighty God, You knew our hearts and knew our fears of death and intimidation, and in Christ You showed us that no power can defeat those whom You hold in Your hand. We praise You, O Lord. In Christ we pray. Amen.

Prayer Of Confession

Lord, we have often been timid and reluctant to stand boldly as witnesses for You because we have feared what others may think or that harm may come to us or our families. Too often, Lord, we have let the world intimidate us or the passage of time cause us to fear. Forgive us, Lord, and help us to proclaim boldly the Good News of eternity! In Christ we pray. Amen.

Hymns

"Victory In Jesus"
"For God So Loved The World"
"Moment By Moment"

Fourth Sunday Of Easter

Second Lesson: Revelation 7:9-17
Theme: Christ is our salvation

Call To Worship

Leader: Sing for joy all who love the Lord, for Christ has brought us life.

People: The resurrection is our promise of life now and through eternity.

Leader: For God will not be defeated by the forces of evil in this world.

People: We rest on the solid rock of God's promise in Christ our Lord.

Leader: Then sing for joy all who love the Lord our God! Sing and give praise!

All: Blessed be the name of the Lord!

Collect

Most wonderful and loving God, You heard our cries and have given us salvation. Help us, O Lord, to share the Good News with every people and nation around the world so all may know Your love. In Christ we pray. Amen.

Prayer Of Confession

Lord, so often we let the cares of the world draw us away from You and the resurrection. The everyday matters worry us so much we act as if You are not real and are not there to be our strength and our shepherd. We try to live life alone, forgetting all You came to teach and give to us. Forgive us, Lord, and lead us home. In Christ we pray. Amen.

Hymns

"Many Gifts, One Spirit"
"In Times Like These"
"In Christ There Is No East Or West"

101

Fourth Sunday Of Easter

Gospel: John 10:22-30
Theme: "My sheep know my voice"

Call To Worship

Leader: Come, let all of God's people give praise and worship the Lord!

People: For the Lord is our Shepherd who watches over us day and night.

Leader: And the Lord guides us through all the days of life to the glory of God.

People: Let no one doubt we are the faithful children of the living God.

Leader: Let us commend for all to hear the loving care of our Good Shepherd!

All: Blessed be the name of the Lord!

Collect

O God, You knew that just as sheep go astray and need a devoted shepherd, we as Your Church would need to be shepherded and guided through the paths of life. We thank You for our Shepherd. In Christ we pray. Amen.

Prayer Of Confession

Lord, we have often tried to live our lives as if You were not there to help and guide us, and usually the results have not been good. Too often we have not even thought to seek Your will for our lives in our times of prayer. Forgive us, Lord, and lead us back into the safety of Your fold so others might see that You are truly our loving Good Shepherd. In Christ we pray. Amen.

Hymns

"Savior, Like A Shepherd Lead Us"
"Just A Closer Walk With Thee"
"Praise Him, Praise Him"

Fifth Sunday Of Easter

First Lesson: Acts 11:1-18
Theme: Christ for the world

Call To Worship

Leader: Celebrate and give thanks, for Christ came to save all nations and tribes!

People: The love of Christ fulfills needs in every heart: Jew or Gentile,

Leader: Male or female, no matter what color or our national language or origins.

People: We are given true life itself in Christ through God's mercy and grace.

Leader: Then let us celebrate not our cultural differences but God's love!

All: Blessed be the name of the Lord!

Collect

O God, in Your infinite wisdom You knew our hearts and our needs and that we were all lost and wandering in the wilderness of sin, and You sent us a Savior. We give You our love and praise. In Christ we pray. Amen.

Prayer Of Confession

Lord, we look upon our salvation as something we deserve because we are worthy. We even begin to think others who are not like us may not be living lives that deserve Your love because of the choices they have made. Forgive us, Lord, and help us to remember that before You cleansed our lives we, too, were not worthy in Your sight. In Christ we pray. Amen.

Hymns

"Christ, For The World We Sing"
"O God Of Every Nation"
"Lead On, O King Eternal"

Fifth Sunday Of Easter

Second Lesson: Revelation 21:1-6
Theme: "I am the Alpha and the Omega"

Call To Worship

Leader: Give praise to the Lord God Almighty, and to Christ our Savior!

People: For our God is the Creator of the Universe and the giver of life.

Leader: In Christ we are given our salvation and life abundant and eternal.

People: As Christ returns, the Church will be a part of God's holy celebration.

Leader: In that day there will no longer be pain or suffering, only God's love.

All: Blessed be the name of the Lord!

Collect

Most loving and merciful God, You are the Great Creator and You alone have sustained the Universe. O God, eternity belongs to You alone. Help us keep our hearts focused on You, Lord. In Christ we pray. Amen.

Prayer Of Confession

O God, with the passing of time we have often allowed the effects of the years to cause us to panic, and we even begin to listen to the world calling us to doubt that You and eternity are real. Forgive us, Lord, and help us move forward with our living witness that the resurrection of Christ was real and that eternity belongs to the faithful in Christ. In Christ we pray. Amen.

Hymns

"How Great Thou Art"
"Morning Has Broken"
"Jesus Paid It All"

Fifth Sunday Of Easter

Gospel: John 13:31-35
Theme: Love one another

Call To Worship

Leader: The power of the Lord is with us this day; let us be glad in it!

People: For God has touched our hearts that we might know life itself.

Leader: Almighty God created the universe and all that is within it,

People: Yet God knows every one of us, even the thoughts of our hearts.

Leader: And even though we fall short of God's will for us, God loves us.

All: Blessed be the name of the Lord!

Collect

O Christ, our wonderful Lord and Savior, You came to teach us what it means to love as You do and to call us to love one another as You first loved us. We praise You, O Lord. In Christ we pray. Amen.

Prayer Of Confession

Lord, so often we forget that You created the universe. We think of You as we are, small and limited, and we think You are too busy to care about our lives. Either way, we miss the message Jesus came to share of Your love and concern for each one of us. Forgive us, Lord, and give us the courage to trust You and to love one another. In Christ we pray. Amen.

Hymns

"Room At The Cross"
"Lord, I Want To Be A Christian"
"Jesus Calls Us"

Sixth Sunday Of Easter

First Lesson: Acts 16:9-15
Theme: Salvation for all who believe

Call To Worship

Leader: Come, let every tongue proclaim the glory of Christ, our Lord and Savior!

People: People in every corner of the world must hear the Good News of Christ.

Leader: For unless they hear, how will they know the joy of the Lord?

People: We are each called by the Lord to share the Gospel we have been given.

Leader: Then let us share the Good News this day in our songs and praise!

All: Blessed be the name of the Lord!

Collect

O Lord, You have called upon each one of us to carry the Gospel of Christ wherever we go with all we meet. Give us the courage to share it freely and the wisdom to share the Gospel effectively. In Christ we pray. Amen.

Prayer Of Confession

Lord, so often we have allowed our lives to settle into mundane routines, and we have forgotten the wonderful message which we are to carry into the world and Your Great Commission calling us to deliver the Good News. Forgive us, Lord, and once again stir our hearts with the joy of Your love so that we may go forth today committed to serving You. In Christ we pray. Amen.

Hymns

"In Times Like These"
"Only Trust Him"
"Living For Jesus"

Sixth Sunday Of Easter

Second Lesson: Revelation 21:10, 22—22:5
Theme: No temple built by hands

Call To Worship

Leader: Come, let us gather together to worship the Lord our God!

People: This is the house of the Lord and it is good that we should be in it.

Leader: But the true temple of God is in the hearts of those who truly believe.

People: In prison camps or in mansions, in poverty or in wealth, we do believe.

Leader: Let our hearts be filled with praise and our voices proclaim God's love!

All: Blessed be the name of the Lord!

Collect

O God, You have called us Your children and to us belongs eternity. No earthly building can house Your greatness, and only in our hearts have You chosen to dwell. We praise You, O Lord. In Christ we pray. Amen.

Prayer Of Confession

Lord, we have allowed ourselves to think of Your Church as the buildings in which we meet, and we have forgotten that You called us to carry the Gospel of Christ into all the world. We have even judged our faithfulness by the quality of the buildings in which we worship, while the hungry and needy have gone unheard. Forgive us, O Lord. In Christ we pray. Amen.

Hymns

"Praise To The Lord, The Almighty"
"Ivory Palaces"
"I'd Rather Have Jesus"

Sixth Sunday Of Easter

Gospel: John 14:23-29
Theme: Keeping the word of Christ

Call To Worship

Leader: The Lord heard our plea and through Christ has sent us a Helper:

People: One who would be our guide and our reminder of all Christ taught us.

Leader: One who would be present in all that we do or wherever we go.

People: One who bears witness of the resurrection and eternity.

Leader: The Holy Spirit is come that we might know the Lord and have life.

All: Blessed be the name of the Lord!

Collect

O merciful and loving God, through Your grace You have called us to know You in Christ and to keep Your word. Empower us, O Lord, to stand firm for You amid the ways of the world around us. In Christ we pray. Amen.

Prayer Of Confession

Lord, we often choose to face life alone and ignore Your Holy Spirit. So often we read in the Scriptures only what we want to read, and we forget Your promises to be with us in every way when we will turn to You. Lord, You want to be with us so much in a living way, help us to trust and open the doors of our hearts to Your presence. In Christ we pray. Amen.

Hymns

"Only Trust Him"
"I Need Thee Every Hour"
"Standing On The Promises"

Ascension Of Our Lord

First Lesson: Acts 1:1-11
Theme: The Ascension

Call To Worship

Leader: Let all who believe in the risen and ascended Christ give praise!

People: It is the Good News, witness of our salvation: Christ lives!

Leader: In Christ God defeated death and the grave, once and for all.

People: In our risen Lord we are called to be the Church, witness to the ages.

Leader: And this same Christ who ascended will, in God's holy time, return.

All: Blessed be the name of the Lord!

Collect

O God, You have given us the message of salvation and the commission to proclaim it in all the world. Strengthen our faith, Lord, that nothing might impede us as Your messengers. In Christ we pray. Amen.

Prayer Of Confession

O God, too often we seem to take for granted some of the awesome events that marked the early years of the Church. We read of saints who died terrible deaths because their commitment was so real they would not deny Your Lordship. Yet so often today our comfort seems more important than our faith in You. Forgive us, Lord, and strengthen us. In Christ we pray. Amen.

Hymns

"All Hail The Power Of Jesus' Name"
"Hail, Thou Once Despised Jesus"
"I Will Sing The Wondrous Story"

Ascension Of Our Lord

Second Lesson: Ephesians 1:15-23
Theme: Christ, the Exalted One

Call To Worship

Leader: Come, let us worship the Lord, the most high exalted of God.

People: Christ, crucified and resurrected, is now at the right hand of God:

Leader: Jesus, who was nailed to the cross that we might have eternal life;

People: Jesus, who was without sin, yet accepted the sins of all time.

Leader: Yet in God's wisdom and mercy it is this same Christ who saves us all.

All: Blessed be the name of the Lord!

Collect

O God, even though as sinners we were rejecting You, in Christ You had the last word and opened the door of salvation to all who would have faith and serve. We praise You, Lord. In Christ we pray. Amen.

Prayer Of Confession

Lord, too often we forget that You sought us out even when we were yet sinners. So often we choose not to remember it was Your love that saved us and not our deserving qualities or nature. Forgive us, Lord, and help us to reach out to others with the same loving and accepting personal openness You so freely extended to us. In Christ we pray. Amen.

Hymns

"O For A Thousand Tongues To Sing"
"Ask Ye What Great Thing I Know"
"My Jesus, I Love Thee"

Ascension Of Our Lord

Gospel: Luke 24:44-53
Theme: The gathering

Call To Worship

Leader: Come, let all who would seek the risen Lord gather now for worship.

People: In Christ we have been promised the Holy Spirit to guide us.

Leader: The Church was established to be God's light in the world.

People: Nothing may prevail against the saving Gospel of Christ.

Leader: Then let all who would serve the risen Christ join in true praise.

All: Blessed be the name of the Lord!

Collect

O God, in Christ You have established Your Church and empowered it to stand even against the gates of Hell. Give us the strength and courage to help lead the way for You, Lord. In Christ we pray. Amen.

Prayer Of Confession

Lord, so often we have listened to the voices of the world that would claim self is all there is to consider in life. Too often we have been unwilling to follow Your example and put the needs and well-being of others first, even as You did in allowing us to nail You to the cross. Forgive us, Lord, and help us more and more to love others. In Christ we pray. Amen.

Hymns

"Shall We Gather At The River"
"We Praise Thee, O God"
"Blest Be The Tie That Binds"

Seventh Sunday Of Easter

First Lesson: Acts 16:16-34
Theme: The power of the Gospel

Call To Worship

Leader: Let the people of God gather this day in praise and thanksgiving!

People: For we were once lost and without hope, but in Christ we found life.

Leader: Christ can change the darkest heart and heal wounds we cannot mend.

People: Christ is the first and the last, and in Christ is our salvation.

Leader: Let us celebrate and give praise to Almighty God who redeemed us all.

All: Blessed be the name of the Lord!

Collect

O God, our Redeemer and Savior, through Your mercy and grace You sent us the Christ and gave us hope, even against the powers of evil. Call us again to carry Your Gospel into all the world. In Christ we pray. Amen.

Prayer Of Confession

Lord, sometimes we have allowed ourselves to feel that we have no recourse against the powers and the influences of evil around us. We have even allowed ourselves to drift into being involved, instead of carrying Your message of grace and redemption to those who desperately need to hear it. Forgive us, Lord, and call us anew to reach the lost. In Christ we pray. Amen.

Hymns

"O God, Our Help In Ages Past"
"The Family Of God"
"How Firm A Foundation"

Seventh Sunday Of Easter

Second Lesson: Revelation 22:12-14, 16-17, 20-21
Theme: The promised return

Call To Worship

Leader: Let us be faithful before the Lord until that day when Christ returns!

People: We have been washed clean through Christ to serve the kingdom of God.

Leader: And we shall be called to account by our Lord and rewarded accordingly.

People: Then let us carry the message of Christ with our words and our deeds.

Leader: And let us celebrate the glory and wonder that is ours in Christ Jesus.

All: Blessed be the name of the Lord!

Collect

Most wonderful God, You have called us to be faithful servants all the days of our lives. In Christ's return, You will know us and call us Your own. We thank You and give You our praise, Lord. In Christ we pray. Amen.

Prayer Of Confession

Lord, sometimes we have lived our lives as if we did not believe Your return would ever come. We have lost our vision of You as the Lord of Eternity and settled for living any way we choose in the days we have, as if we will never be held to account for our choices. Forgive us, Lord, and call us anew to be faithful until that days in which You return. In Christ we pray. Amen.

Hymns

"Come, Thou Long Expected Jesus"
"Sweet By And By"
"It Is Well With My Soul"

Seventh Sunday Of Easter

Gospel: John 17:20-26
Theme: We are one with Christ

Call To Worship

Leader: Lord, where are You in this world so full of modern technology?

People: Lord, where are You in the midst of our personal confusion?

Leader: Lord, where are You when the world around us seems to be crumbling?

People: Lord, where shall we look to find Your presence in our day?

Leader: Christ is truly with us always. Stand sure on your faith in God!

All: Blessed be the name of the Lord!

Collect

Almighty Creator God, You laid the foundations of the Universe itself and yet You desire to walk with us in every day of our lives. We give You our praise and our heartfelt love. In Christ we pray. Amen.

Prayer Of Confession

Lord, we are so blind sometimes when we need to see You most. In our distress we fail to see Your wonders around us, Your love in the caring of those who reach out to help us, and Your guidance in helping us work things out in our daily lives. Forgive us for being so blind. Help us not only to see but also to be Your presence in today's world. In Christ we pray. Amen.

Hymns

"Open My Eyes, That I May See"
"What A Friend We Have In Jesus"
"It Is Well With My Soul"

Pentecost

First Lesson: Acts 2:1-21
Theme: Receiving the Holy Spirit

Call To Worship
Leader: Let us come together and celebrate the presence of the Holy Spirit!

People: For when we have been weak, the Holy Spirit has sustained us.

Leader: When we have journeyed in Christ's name, the Spirit has guided us.

People: When we were sick or in harm's way, the Spirit of the Lord was with us.

Leader: When we have sought understanding and wisdom, God's Spirit led us.

All: Blessed be the name of the Lord!

Collect
Almighty Creator of the Universe, we are so blessed by Your gift of the Holy Spirit to guide and walk with us in every moment of life. We thank and praise You, O Lord. In Christ we pray. Amen.

Prayer Of Confession
Lord, we have a tendency to take on the stresses and strains of life completely on our own and ignore Your gift of prayer and the Holy Spirit. We even reach our breaking point, yet we refuse to seek Your help and Your will for our lives. Forgive us, Lord, and help us have the strength to submit our wills to Yours. In Christ we pray. Amen.

Hymns
"Breathe On Me, Breath Of God"
"Cleanse Me"
"Sweet, Sweet Spirit"

Pentecost

Second Lesson: Romans 8:14-17
Theme: Adoption not slavery

Call To Worship
Leader: Let all who celebrate God's love and mercy gather now for worship!

People: In Christ, God has called us to be adopted children in the kingdom.

Leader: We are heirs of the kingdom and all the wonders of eternity.

People: As God's children we receive correction and nurture in the Lord.

Leader: We have much to celebrate and much to share with all the world.

All: Blessed be the name of the Lord!

Collect
Almighty God, after the cross You could have easily found us wanting and unworthy of Your Love, yet instead You called us to receive adoption and eternity. We give You our love and praise. In Christ we pray. Amen.

Prayer Of Confession
Lord, so often we have failed to be the responsible children You would have us be. By adoption You made us part of Your family, yet we have too often lived in ways hardly befitting the children of God. We have not faithfully shared Your love with others nor have we been quick to help those in need. Forgive us, Lord, and help us remember daily that we live in Your name. In Christ we pray. Amen.

Hymns
"A Child Of The King"
"Christ For The World We Sing"
"This Is My Father's World"

116

Pentecost

Gospel: John 14:8-17 (25-27)
Theme: Empowered by the Holy Spirit

Call To Worship

Leader: Let us come together, all whose lives would proclaim God's glory!

People: We open our hearts this day to God's presence and power.

Leader: In our prayers we lift all that we are before the Lord.

People: With courage we will do and share God's love with the world.

Leader: Let our voices be raised in praise and song to the glory of God!

All: Blessed be the name of the Lord!

Collect

O God, You alone are to be praised. We sought Your mercy, and You also extended Your grace. We seek to serve You, and You empower us with Your gifts. Fill us, O Lord, with Your presence. In Christ we pray. Amen.

Prayer Of Confession

Lord, we often fail to bring our concerns before You in prayer. We all but deny Your power simply because we will not pray and let Your will be done in our lives. Forgive us, Lord, and help us to open our hearts with courage to Your presence so that the whole world might know that Your love and grace are real. In Christ we pray. Amen.

Hymns

"O Spirit Of The Living God"
"God Of Grace And God Of Glory"
"Holy, Holy, Holy"

First Sunday After Pentecost
(Holy Trinity)

First Lesson: Proverbs 8:1-4, 22-31
Theme: The wisdom of the Lord

Call To Worship

Leader: Let us gather together, for we are the Church of the Lord Jesus Christ!

People: Throughout the ages we have stood strong to proclaim Christ's love.

Leader: And in the face of evil God's wisdom has guided us to victory.

People: In daily living the Holy Spirit has brought the wisdom of God for life.

Leader: Then let us celebrate the wonderful nature of God's loving grace.

All: Blessed be the name of the Lord!

Collect

Most loving and gracious God, through the Holy Spirit You have given us a helper and make Your wisdom available to all who will seek Your presence in their lives. We thank You, O Lord. In Christ we pray. Amen.

Prayer Of Confession

Lord, like children we have often chosen to live our lives on our own and not seek the help and guidance You offer us in the Holy Spirit. We have even thought our wisdom adequate for life and not sought Your help in prayer. Forgive us, Lord, and give us the wisdom and courage to seek Your help to live as You would have us live. In Christ we pray. Amen.

Hymns

"Spirit Of The Living God"
"Guide Me, O Thou Great Jehovah"
"Be Thou My Vision"

First Sunday After Pentecost
(Holy Trinity)

Second Lesson: Romans 5:1-5
Theme: Through trials to hope

Call To Worship

Leader: Let us gather and give praise to the Lord God Almighty!

People: Our God called Abraham and Sarah and made of them a nation.

Leader: And in the days of Pharaoh, God led Moses to free the Hebrew Children.

People: Our God is mighty and wonderful and will sustain us against all evil.

Leader: In our trials and tribulations let us cling to the promises of God.

All: Blessed be the name of the Lord!

Collect

O God, in Your infinite wisdom You have always called to us and gently touched our hearts with Your love. Give us the spiritual eyes to see and the ears to hear Your word in today's world. In Christ we pray. Amen.

Prayer Of Confession

Lord, sometimes amid the problems and challenges of life today we fail to seek Your guidance and choose to lean only on our own resources. Too often, Lord, only when matters have become impossible have we turned to You and sought Your help. Forgive us, Lord, and help us remember Your promise to be with us each step of our lives, if we will but come to You. In Christ we pray. Amen.

Hymns

"Amazing Grace"
"Redeemed"
"God Will Take Care Of You"

First Sunday After Pentecost
(Holy Trinity)

Gospel: John 16:12-15
Theme: The work of the Holy Spirit

Call To Worship

Leader: The Lord is with us; we are not alone.

People: The Lord goes with us in our daily journey through life.

Leader: The Lord goes before us to face all who would bring us harm.

People: The Lord would shine through us so that all might see God's love.

Leader: The Lord is with us so that our lives might sing out in praise to God!

All: Blessed be the name of the Lord!

Collect

O God, in Your infinite wisdom You have given us the Holy Spirit to touch our lives and to teach us Your wonderful ways. Give us the ears to listen and the wisdom to live for You. In Christ we pray. Amen.

Prayer Of Confession

Lord, we often act and live as though You did not send the Holy Spirit to be with us. We fail to pray, we fail to hear Your word, and we fail to reach out and share You with those around us. Lord, forgive us when our lives fail to proclaim Your love and mercy for all the world to hear. Help us to share the Gospel with all who are around us. In Christ we pray. Amen.

Hymns

"Come, Thou Almighty King"
"Open My Eyes, That I May See"
"I Surrender All"

Proper 4
Sunday between May 29 and June 4 inclusive

First Lesson: 1 Kings 18:20-39
Theme: God knows no equal!

Call To Worship

Leader: Come this day and enter the house of the Lord for worship and praise!

People: Our God has no equal and cannot be matched in all the universe.

Leader: Yet throughout the ages we have made other gods and held them most high.

People: All we like sheep have gone astray, yet our God leads us home with love.

Leader: God is mighty and knows no equal and God's love is worthy of our praise.

All: Blessed be the name of the Lord!

Collect

Most loving and merciful God, throughout creation You have demonstrated Your infinite power, yet in Christ You have extended to us Your saving mercy and grace. We give You our love and praise. In Christ we pray. Amen.

Prayer Of Confession

Lord, so often without truly thinking we have allowed the things of this world to become our focus of worship, and we have turned away from You. Sometimes we have even sought the guidance of spiritual powers which You have forbidden us to seek. Forgive us, Lord, and guide us back into Your fold. Use our lives to lead others into Your holy kingdom. In Christ we pray. Amen.

Hymns

"Majesty, Worship His Majesty"
"Jesus, We Just Want To Thank You"
"Love, Mercy, And Grace"

Proper 4
Sunday between May 29 and June 4 inclusive

Second Lesson: Galatians 1:1-12
Theme: Our message is Christ and Christ only

Call To Worship

Leader: Let all who trust in Christ as their Lord and Savior come now for worship.

People: In Christ alone do we have salvation and the promise of eternal life.

Leader: Not by our works or even by our piety are we saved,

People: But by God's mercy and grace and through our faith in the Lord.

Leader: Let our hearts bring forth praise and our voices proclaim Christ.

All: Blessed be the name of the Lord!

Collect

O God, in Your wonderful mercy You sent Christ so that we might have salvation. Give us the strength and the courage to carry the message of Christ to every heart and every nation in the world. In Christ we pray. Amen.

Prayer Of Confession

Lord, like the people of Galatia we have accepted Your salvation only to turn away and chase after the desires of our hearts. Instead of being faithful followers proclaiming the Good News, we have lived as though You had never touched our lives. Forgive us, Lord, and call us again so that we may once more serve You with love and praise. In Christ we pray. Amen.

Hymns

"He Is Lord"
"He Touched Me"
"Wonderful Words Of Life"

Proper 4
Sunday between May 29 and June 4 inclusive

Gospel: Luke 7:1-10
Theme: Faith beyond ourselves

Call To Worship

Leader: Come, all who would walk by faith; gather in the house of the Lord!

People: We are called by Christ to give witness to God's love and power.

Leader: We are called to proclaim to a doubting world that Christ truly lives!

People: In our hearts and in our lives the message of God's mercy rings true.

Leader: Then let us raise our voices as one in adoration and song!

All: Blessed be the name of the Lord!

Collect

Most loving and gracious Lord, You have called us to have faith in You even when the world around us denies that any hope exists. Touch our hearts anew, Lord, and fill us with Your joy and hope. In Christ we pray. Amen.

Prayer Of Confession

Lord, so often when we are faced with the stresses and strains of life, our faith falters and we turn away from You, depending on our own resources to find solutions. Even in the easy times we tend to celebrate our good fortune without praising You as well. Forgive us, Lord, and lead us to walk daily in Your will. In Christ we pray. Amen.

Hymns

"I Will Sing The Wondrous Story"
"Blessed Be The Name"
"The Family Of God"

Proper 5
Sunday between June 5 and June 11 inclusive

First Lesson: 1 Kings 17:8-24
Theme: The Lord is our Provider

Call To Worship

Leader: The Lord our God is mighty and wonderful!

People: And greatly to be praised by all who know the joy of God's grace.

Leader: God is our sustainer and provider and touches our lives every day.

People: In Christ we have been called to be numbered among the children of God.

Leader: Let us worship and give praise to our loving and merciful God!

All: Blessed be the name of the Lord!

Collect

Almighty God, Creator of the Universe, in Your infinite love You have sustained Your faithful servants throughout the ages. Sustain us, Lord, as we carry the Gospel of Christ to the world. In Christ we pray. Amen.

Prayer Of Confession

Lord, at times we have been very slow to acknowledge that it is You who sustains our lives and not our own labors or even the wealth of the world around us. It is by Your hand that the sun shines, the wind blows, and the rains are plenty. Yet too often we think it is only by our own efforts and wisdom that we have food. Forgive us, Lord, and help us celebrate Your love. In Christ we pray. Amen.

Hymns

"His Eye Is On The Sparrow"
"Hymn Of Promise"
"Praise Him, Praise Him"

124

Proper 5
Sunday between June 5 and June 11 inclusive

Second Lesson: Galatians 1:11-24
Theme: The glory of God's redeemed

Call To Worship

Leader: Give praise to the Lord, for in Christ we have been redeemed!

People: Even when we were yet sinners and rebelling against God, we were loved.

Leader: And through Christ, the love of God has transformed our hearts.

People: As once we rebelled, we now join the celebration of God's wonderful love.

Leader: The change in our hearts gives glorious witness that the Gospel is true.

All: Blessed be the name of the Lord!

Collect

Almighty God, we celebrate the way in which You firmly but gently change each heart and move us ever closer to the ways of Christ. We praise You and openly give You our faith and love. In Christ we pray. Amen.

Prayer Of Confession

Lord, so often we have failed to realize the wonderful ways You use our lives as living witnesses to Your Gospel. We have felt that it is only our words that tell of Christ, and we have failed to see that each time we allow Your love to flow through us to touch others our testimony has been real. Forgive us, Lord, and help us be more faithful followers. In Christ we pray. Amen.

Hymns

"Love Lifted Me"
"Blessed Assurance"
"Jesus Paid It All"

Proper 5
Sunday between June 5 and June 11 inclusive

Gospel: Luke 7:11-17
Theme: Christ who conquers even death

Call To Worship

Leader: Let us lift our voices in praise and worship before the Lord!

People: We worship and praise the Lord of the living and not of the dead.

Leader: For in Christ death has lost its sting, and we will not be afraid.

People: Jesus raised the dead and gives eternal life to all who believe.

Leader: Truly let us sing praise for the mercy and glory of God's love.

All: Blessed be the name of the Lord!

Collect

Most wonderful Lord and Savior, You are the Almighty One and even death must bow to Your will. Give us the faith to stand firm as Your people for the world to see even in the face of death. In Christ we pray. Amen.

Prayer Of Confession

Lord, so often we tend to hear only the words of fear and death around us, and we do not proclaim Your truth. Too often we fear the pain and rejection of the world and forget that those who do Your will are promised eternity. Open our spirits, Lord, and help us keep our focus on You so that we might stand firm and give witness to Your eternal life. In Christ we pray. Amen.

Hymns

"Lead Me To Calvary"
"Ask Ye What Great Thing I Know"
"Praise Him, Praise Him"

Proper 6
Sunday between June 12 and June 18 inclusive

First Lesson: 1 Kings 21:1-21a
Theme: Evil will not prevail against the Lord

Call To Worship

Leader: Stand firm before the Lord! The powers of this world cannot prevail!

People: Yet the world is powerful and does threaten great harm to God's people.

Leader: But the powers of this age do not control our faith or our eternity.

People: We stand on the Word of the Lord! Christ is the rock of our salvation!

Leader: So that all the world should hear, let us give praise and glory to our God!

All: Blessed be the name of the Lord!

Collect

Almighty and wonderful God, even though all the powers of evil might raise their hand against You, Your Holy Kingdom will be victorious. Call us anew into Your service, O Lord. In Christ we pray. Amen.

Prayer Of Confession

Lord, sometimes amid all that seems to be going wrong in the world around us we have been tempted to doubt that You really are in control of our destiny. At times we have even considered yielding to pressures that would have us do things You would not have us be about. Forgive us, Lord, and instill in our hearts the strength to be Your faithful servants. In Christ we pray. Amen.

Hymns

"All Hail The Power Of Jesus' Name"
"He Keeps Me Singing"
"Standing On The Promises"

Proper 6
Sunday between June 12 and June 18 inclusive

Second Lesson: Galatians 2:15-21
Theme: Living by faith

Call To Worship

Leader: Come, let all whose faith is in Christ gather now for worship!

People: We begin each day only by God's wonderful mercy and grace.

Leader: And our labors are dedicated to the Lord, who has saved us from sin.

People: We come to the end of each day with the Lord, who has walked with us.

Leader: We have true life and joy only in Christ and the love of our God!

All: Blessed be the name of the Lord!

Collect

Most wonderful and gracious God, You are truly the Almighty One, yet in Your mercy You have chosen to walk with even the least of us through all the days of our lives. We praise You, O Lord. In Christ we pray. Amen.

Prayer Of Confession

Lord, it has often been difficult for us to move beyond what we can see and touch and to step out in faith to be about the things You would have us do in Your name. Too often, Lord, we allow ourselves to be enchanted by the comforts of life, as we fail to remember that we must walk in faith to know Your eternity. Forgive us, Lord, and call us again to serve You. In Christ we pray. Amen.

Hymns

"Great Is Thy Faithfulness"
"Have Faith In God"
"My Faith Looks Up To Thee"

Proper 6
Sunday between June 12 and June 18 inclusive

Gospel: Luke 7:36—8:3
Theme: Forgiven before the Lord

Call To Worship

Leader: Come, all who have sinned and fallen short of the glory of God!

People: But the house of the Lord is only for the righteous.

Leader: In Christ, we are each made righteous before the Lord.

People: Are we washed clean and made pure so as not to offend our God?

Leader: Lift your voices in praise! In Christ, we are pure before God.

All: Blessed be the name of the Lord!

Collect

Most perfect and mighty God, even when we were mired in the depths of our sins You reached out to us, pulled us free, and washed us clean. Help us to proclaim Your love for all the world to hear. In Christ we pray. Amen.

Prayer Of Confession

Lord, so often the condemnation of the world and even of our own hearts blinds us to the price You paid to take our sins away. We are so accustomed to the ways of our culture that we will not see we have each fallen very short of Your standards for us. Forgive us, Lord, and help us to accept Your forgiveness so that we might pass it on. In Christ we pray. Amen.

Hymns

"Grace Greater Than Our Sin"
"Are Ye Able?"
"Jesus Paid It All"

129

Proper 7
Sunday between June 19 and June 25 inclusive

First Lesson: 1 Kings 19:1-15a
Theme: Faithful to the voice of God

Call To Worship

Leader: Come now and let us gather in the house of the Lord for worship!

People: In all our days the Lord has been our guide and our salvation.

Leader: The Lord God Almighty has faithfully walked with us since the days of old.

People: Even the mighty kings of the world cannot stop the Word of the Lord!

Leader: God is truly worthy of our praise and our never ending love.

All: Blessed be the name of the Lord!

Collect

Most loving and merciful God, through Your wonderful grace You have always reached out to us even before we understood our sins, and You gently call us to follow Your Word. Help us hear, O Lord. In Christ we pray. Amen.

Prayer Of Confession

Lord, amid the thunderous noise of our everyday world we have seldom taken the time to be still and hear Your Word. Too often, we have acted as if we were afraid to seek the silence that would allow our hearts to hear the still, small voice in which You call to us. Forgive us, O God, and give us the courage to stop and hear You. In Christ we pray. Amen.

Hymns

"Where He Leads Me"
"Fairest Lord Jesus"
"Have Thine Own Way, Lord"

Proper 7
Sunday between June 19 and June 25 inclusive

Second Lesson: Galatians 3:23-29
Theme: Faith stands beyond the Law

Call To Worship
Leader: Come, all who love the Lord so that we might worship together!

People: Let us come together and share all the Lord has done.

Leader: Let our voices be lifted in praise and prayer before the Lord.

People: For once we were under the law until the Lord led us to faith.

Leader: Let us come together to sing and give praise to God.

All: Blessed be the name of the Lord!

Collect
O God, we are grateful that You came so we might know the faith and hope that makes life so rich and full. Lord, give us the courage to seek Your will for our lives and the faith to pursue it. In Christ we pray. Amen.

Prayer Of Confession
Lord, we often forget who we are and that You touched our lives and made us messengers to the world. Instead we go our own ways and seek only our own interests. Forgive us, we ask, O Lord, and give us the courage and the strength to declare Your message of love and mercy to all those around us. In Christ we pray. Amen.

Hymns
"How Firm A Foundation"
"Nearer, My God, To Thee"
"He Touched Me"

Proper 7
Sunday between June 19 and June 25 inclusive

Gospel: Luke 8:26-39
Theme: Victorious over the powers of evil

Call To Worship
Leader: Let us celebrate the victory of our Lord over all the forces of evil!

People: In the resurrection of Christ, God wrought a mighty victory over death.

Leader: And every entity of evil knows the power of our Lord Jesus Christ.

People: Let our hearts not be afraid and our faith in Christ remain strong.

Leader: One day every knee will indeed bow before Christ our Lord and Savior.

All: Blessed be the name of the Lord!

Collect
O God, the Universe knows You are without equal and humbly bows before You. Give us the courage and power to carry Your message of hope and love into the world, sharing it without fear. In Christ we pray. Amen.

Prayer Of Confession
Lord, so often in our modern world we have felt ourselves so sophisticated and technically advanced that we have forgotten You are the only true source of knowledge and power in the Universe. Sometimes we even allow ourselves to believe that the forces of evil are not real unless we can see them face to face. Forgive us, Lord, and surround us with Your love. In Christ we pray. Amen.

Hymns
"Holy, Holy, Holy"
"Lift High The Cross"
"All Hail The Power Of Jesus' Name"

Proper 8
Sunday between June 26 and July 2 inclusive

First Lesson: 2 Kings 2:1-2, 6-14
Theme: Prophets of the Lord

Call To Worship

Leader: Let all who would proclaim the word of the Lord gather now for worship!

People: We have heard the Good News of Christ, and we would share it with the world.

Leader: Let us carry Christ to every nation and to every people on Earth.

People: Only as we share Christ will others come to know God's salvation.

Leader: Then let our hearts be joyful as we boldly proclaim the risen Christ.

All: Blessed be the name of the Lord!

Collect

O God, in Your wonderful mercy and grace You have honored us to be among Your family. As Your children, You have called us to spread the Gospel of Christ for all to hear. We praise You, Lord. In Christ we pray. Amen.

Prayer Of Confession

Lord, so often when You have called us to carry Your word into the world we have not been willing to stand boldly for You. We have even refused to be different because people might notice us and think us strange. Forgive us, Lord, and call us again to proclaim Your Good News of salvation in Christ in every land and to every people. In Christ we pray. Amen.

Hymns

"Here I Am, Lord"
"Christ For The World We Sing"
"We've A Story To Tell To The Nations"

133

Proper 8
Sunday between June 26 and July 2 inclusive

Second Lesson: Galatians 5:1, 13-25
Theme: The freedom of God's love

Call To Worship

Leader: Let us lift our voices in praise to God for our redemption!

People: We were once bound not only by sin but also by the yoke of the Law.

Leader: But Christ has called us to freedom that we might truly love one another.

People: In Christ the Law became alive as we work for peace and harmony.

Leader: Then let us celebrate our freedom in wonderful song and praise to God!

All: Blessed be the name of the Lord!

Collect

O God, in Your infinite wisdom You gave us freedom so that we might truly know Your love and share it with others. Help us use our freedom wisely, Lord, to help and care for our neighbors. In Christ we pray. Amen.

Prayer Of Confession

O God, too often we have not remembered the price You paid for our freedom. At times we have so taken our freedom for granted that we have sought only the desires of our hearts and we have not loved one another or cared for our neighbors as ourselves so that we might know Your peace or the wonderful joys of life You meant us to have. Forgive us, Lord. In Christ we pray. Amen.

Hymns

"Jesu, Jesu"
"Let There Be Peace On Earth"
"Wonderful Peace"

Proper 8
Sunday between June 26 and July 2 inclusive

Gospel: Luke 9:51-62
Theme: Follow first the Lord

Call To Worship

Leader: Let us gather together and give praise to the Lord!

People: We would serve the Lord wherever God would send us.

Leader: Christ has called us to carry the Gospel to every part of the earth.

People: But life's demands are heavy and we have much yet to do this day!

Leader: Only those who serve Christ first can truly know the Kingdom of God.

All: Blessed be the name of the Lord!

Collect

Almighty Creator God, in the midst of the rushing world around us You have called us to hear Your voice and to follow You. Give us ears to hear and strength to follow faithfully. In Christ we pray. Amen.

Prayer Of Confession

Lord, so often we let everyday life come before Your call on our lives. We get so busy with the routine matters that we fail to hear Your call to share the Gospel. Forgive us, Lord. Give us the ears to hear the cries for help and the eyes to see those around us in need, that in reaching out we might truly be Your Church today. In Christ we pray. Amen.

Hymns

"O Jesus, I Have Promised"
"He Is Lord"
"Jesus Calls Us O'er The Tumult"

Proper 9
Sunday between July 3 and July 9 inclusive

First Lesson: 2 Kings 5:1-14
Theme: The Word of the Lord restores us

Call To Worship

Leader: Praise be to the Lord, for we are each one restored by God's Holy Word.

People: Not by the words of our wisdom or by our deeds, but in Christ our Lord.

Leader: Indeed the Word of the Lord has restored our souls and made us whole.

People: Each one of us is a personal witness of the power and love of God.

Leader: Let us lift our voices together in praise to Christ our Lord and Savior.

All: Blessed be the name of the Lord!

Collect

Eternal and Almighty God, we read in Your Scriptures of the wonderful way You restored the ancient ones, and we desire in our hearts to know Your healing power in our land today. Restore us, O Lord. In Christ we pray. Amen.

Prayer Of Confession

Lord, as is so common today, we have often sought our restoration in our own technologies and understandings, and we have failed to seek You. When all other avenues of help have failed, only then do we turn to You. Forgive us, Lord, and give us the courage to seek Your leadership and guidance first in our lives and not just as a last resort. In Christ we pray. Amen.

Hymns

"Since Jesus Came Into My Heart"
"Turn Your Eyes Upon Jesus"
"I Know Whom I Have Believed"

Proper 9
Sunday between July 3 and July 9 inclusive

Second Lesson: Galatians 6:(1-6) 7-16
Theme: Sow in the Spirit

Call To Worship

Leader: Let us lift our voices in praise to Almighty God, for Christ is risen!

People: No longer need we fear death nor are the world's standards ours.

Leader: For we are called to live by the love of Christ without fear.

People: Christ holds our eternity and no other force can take it from us.

Leader: Then let us live boldly for Christ, for we are servants of Almighty God!

All: Blessed be the name of the Lord!

Collect

Most wonderful and loving God, in Your wonderful wisdom You have shown us that if we expect to receive Your eternity, we must sow our seed not in the world but with You. We praise You, Lord. In Christ we pray. Amen.

Prayer Of Confession

O God, sometimes we have not remembered Your warning that we will reap what we sow, and we have sown our crops not in eternity but in fields of this world. Instead of abiding by Your word, we have chosen to live "our own way" and we have been sorrowed by the harvest we receive. Forgive us, Lord, and lead us again to sow in Your wonderful fields. In Christ we pray. Amen.

Hymns

"Bringing In The Sheaves"
"Joyful, Joyful, We Adore Thee"
"Sweet, Sweet Spirit"

137

Proper 9
Sunday between July 3 and July 9 inclusive

Gospel: Luke 10:1-11, 16-20
Theme: "The harvest is plentiful"

Call To Worship

Leader: The fields are ripe for harvest, but who will reap for the Lord?

People: Let each one who has known God's mercy and grace now serve the Lord.

Leader: Truly only those who know the living Lord can lead the lost to salvation.

People: Then let our hearts be resolute that we shall carry Christ to the world!

Leader: And let our hearts be filled with joy for each who receives the Lord!

All: Blessed be the name of the Lord!

Collect

O God, You are the Lord of the harvest and we are so honored that You have called us to help in the task. Give us the strength and the courage to share faithfully Your Gospel. In Christ we pray. Amen.

Prayer Of Confession

Lord, You have called upon us to share Your wonderful salvation with those around us, but we have often been reluctant or we have been "too busy." We have let the opinions others might have about us keep us from boldly sharing Your love. Forgive us, Lord, and fill us anew with Your presence. Send us again to proclaim Your Gospel to the world. In Christ we pray. Amen.

Hymns

"Softly And Tenderly"
"Count Your Blessings"
"This Is My Father's World"

Proper 10
Sunday between July 10 and July 16 inclusive

First Lesson: Amos 7:7-17
Theme: Held to the plumb; true and straight

Call To Worship

Leader: Let the people of God gather now for praise and worship!

People: Let our voices ring out together in joyful song and exaltations to God,

Leader: And let our lives be found true and faithful before our Lord and Savior.

People: Through our lives others may come to see the witness of Christ our Lord.

Leader: Let all who witness our praise know how much we love our Lord and Savior.

All: Blessed be the name of the Lord!

Collect

Most wonderful and merciful God, in Your wisdom You have called us to become members of Your family. Just as our children need guidance, we also need Yours. Keep us on Your paths, O Lord. In Christ we pray. Amen.

Prayer Of Confession

Lord, sometimes we complain the loudest as we face Your loving discipline when all we really want is to do things our own way. Too often, Lord, we seem as heirs in Your kingdom to have forgotten that we must live in a manner true to the Master we serve. Forgive us, Lord, and always lead us back to the true standards You would have us witness in the world. In Christ we pray. Amen.

Hymns

"O God Of Every Nation"
"Happy The Home When God Is There"
"Open My Eyes, That I May See"

139

Proper 10
Sunday between July 10 and July 16 inclusive

Second Lesson: Colossians 1:1-14
Theme: Let us be fruitful!

Call To Worship

Leader: We come together as heirs to the Kingdom of God.
People: We come together with joy and thanksgiving.
Leader: We come together to proclaim God's grace that made us whole.
People: We come together to celebrate that we are indeed part of God's family.
Leader: We come together to shout praise for God's loving mercy and grace.
All: Blessed be the name of the Lord!

Collect

O God, You have made us Your own and called us to bring forth the fruit of Your presence in our lives so that all the world will know Your kingdom is real. We praise You, O Lord. In Christ we pray. Amen.

Prayer Of Confession

Lord, so many times we have failed to remember that we are members of and heirs to Your Kingdom. Instead, we have acted as though we live in our own little kingdoms and have focused on our own little worlds. Forgive us, Lord, and help us to reach out and share with a hurting world the love we receive by being Your subjects. In Christ we pray. Amen.

Hymns

"I Love Thy Kingdom, Lord"
"Make Me A Blessing"
"I Am Thine, O Lord"

Proper 10
Sunday between July 10 and July 16 inclusive

Gospel: Luke 10:25-37
Theme: What is a Good Neighbor? (The Good Samaritan)

Call To Worship

Leader: May the love of Christ be with you as we gather now for worship!

People: And may the love of Christ be with you also in this service of praise!

Leader: Let our worship go beyond these walls in our caring for all we meet in need.

People: Let our hearts celebrate Christ as we serve the Lord with gladness!

Leader: Let all we do for others bring glory and honor to Christ's name!

All: Blessed be the name of the Lord!

Collect

Most loving and merciful God, in Your wonderful love You have called us to love and care for others just as we would love ourselves. Give us the strength, Lord, to keep Your charge. In Christ we pray. Amen.

Prayer Of Confession

Lord, so often we have allowed ourselves to focus mainly on our own desires, and we pass by those who desperately need our help. Too often, Lord, we have allowed ourselves to become comfortable in the world, as we totally ignore the voices of the needy calling for our help just to survive. Forgive us, Lord, and help us make a real difference for You today. In Christ we pray. Amen.

Hymns

"Freely, Freely"
"Are Ye Able?"
"Take My Life, And Let It Be"

Proper 11
Sunday between July 17 and July 23 inclusive

First Lesson: Amos 8:1-12
Theme: God's judgment comes

Call To Worship
Leader: Let us enter the house of the Lord with gladness and praise!

People: For the Lord our God is just and righteous and will not be deceived.

Leader: Let all who would tempt the Lord hear that God's justice is swift.

People: None shall stand against the Lord, from the greatest to the least.

Leader: Yet God has been merciful, and we have received in Christ God's grace.

All: Blessed be the name of the Lord!

Collect
Most righteous and just God, You call us daily to know Your will so that we may avoid Your judgment. Lord, give us the ears to hear and the wisdom to follow Your Word. In Christ we pray. Amen.

Prayer Of Confession
Lord, so often we have taken Your mercy and grace for granted, as if Your judgment could never come. We have even allowed ourselves to doubt that You would ever call us to account for our lives and decisions. Forgive us, Lord, and help us to draw ever closer to being the loving people You created us to be so the world might know that Your Gospel is true. In Christ we pray. Amen.

Hymns
"Come, Thou Fount Of Every Blessing"
"Make Me A Captive, Lord"
"O Master, Let Me Walk With Thee"

Proper 11
Sunday between July 17 and July 23 inclusive

Second Lesson: Colossians 1:15-28
Theme: Reconciled in Christ

Call To Worship

Leader: Let all the world hear our praise and thanksgiving for God's mercy!

People: For only in Christ are we redeemed and do we know God's salvation.

Leader: In the cross and the resurrection we are reconciled with the Lord.

People: Our Lord died for our sins so that we might have eternal life and joy.

Leader: Let our hearts give praise to God for mercy and grace beyond our sin.

All: Blessed be the name of the Lord!

Collect

Most loving and merciful God, in Your infinite wisdom You sent Christ to be our Savior even before we understood how deeply we were stained with sin. We praise You, O Lord. In Christ we pray. Amen.

Prayer Of Confession

Lord, so often we try to earn our salvation with works or the gifts of our labors, and we fail to accept Your mercy and grace. We have allowed ourselves to think that if we work harder or keep the law more closely somehow we will actually deserve Your love. We often seem unable to grasp that You love us because You are love itself. Forgive us, Lord. In Christ we pray. Amen.

Hymns

"Standing On The Promises"
"Grace Greater Than Our Sin"
"Have Thine Own Way, Lord"

Proper 11
Sunday between July 17 and July 23 inclusive

Gospel: Luke 10:38-42
Theme: Perfection or grace?

Call To Worship

Leader: We come together to worship, laying aside the burdens of this world.

People: And we set aside the pressures of daily life so that we may worship God.

Leader: We let go of our personal goals to be perfect and accept God's love.

People: We give up all that we are so that we might truly know life in Christ.

Leader: Let us celebrate and give praise for the true life God has given us.

All: Blessed be the name of the Lord!

Collect

Most wonderful and loving God, through the life of Christ we have come to see we are Yours through mercy and grace and not through our personal perfection. Help us to share Your Gospel, Lord. In Christ we pray. Amen.

Prayer Of Confession

Lord, so many times we have sought to earn Your acceptance and failed to accept Your grace and mercy. We have tried to do all the "right" things, and failed to love and care for each other or even ourselves. Forgive us, Lord, and give us the courage and the strength to accept Your unmerited love and grace and to share them with others. In Christ we pray. Amen.

Hymns

"Love, Mercy, And Grace"
"Amazing Grace"
"God Of Grace And God Of Glory"

Proper 12
Sunday between July 24 and July 30 inclusive

First Lesson: Hosea 1:2-10
Theme: "Not My People" (RSV)

Call To Worship
Leader: The Lord is our salvation, and we will worship no other gods!

People: No other power in all the universe can compare to Almighty God.

Leader: But many have strayed to worship the things and powers of this world.

People: Our God will not be mocked, yet God's justice is tempered by mercy.

Leader: Mercy extended to us through the redeeming love of Christ.

All: Blessed be the name of the Lord!

Collect
Merciful and gracious God, even when we have broken our covenant with You, You have never given up on reclaiming us for Your own. Lord, give us the wisdom to seek again Your redeeming love. In Christ we pray. Amen.

Prayer Of Confession
Lord, we often allow ourselves to drift far away from the sort of lives You would have us live. Too often, we have not seen how the choices we make either close You out of our lives or totally compromise our witness for You. Forgive us, Lord, and give us the strength and the courage to be faithful and true witnesses of Your love. In Christ we pray. Amen.

Hymns
"Take My Life And Let It Be"
"Love, Mercy, And Grace"
"Abide With Me"

145

Proper 12
Sunday between July 24 and July 30 inclusive

Second Lesson: Colossians 2:6-15 (16-19)
Theme: Living in Christ

Call To Worship

Leader: Let all who know Christ as their Lord and Savior come now for worship.

People: We have been redeemed through the cross and the resurrection of Christ.

Leader: Not by any other name have we known God's wonderful salvation.

People: Only in Christ have we known the joy and peace of God in our hearts.

Leader: Then let us share the message of Christ with all who will listen.

All: Blessed be the name of the Lord!

Collect

Almighty and loving God, through Christ You have given us the gift of life itself so that we might share the Good News with all we meet. Restore our souls, Lord, and keep our message pure. In Christ we pray. Amen.

Prayer Of Confession

Lord, at times we have taken the wonderful blessing of Your presence in our lives for granted, and we have forgotten that many have neither heard the Good News of Christ nor experienced firsthand the joy and peace of Your presence in their lives. Forgive us, Lord, and help us to be more sensitive to the needs of others in sharing Your precious Gospel. In Christ we pray. Amen.

Hymns

"Living For Jesus"
"I Surrender All"
"We've A Story To Tell To The Nations"

Proper 12
Sunday between July 24 and July 30 inclusive

Gospel: Luke 11:1-13
Theme: The importance of prayer

Call To Worship

Leader: We gather together in Christ as part of the family of God.

People: We bring our sorrows and our joys, our trials and our accomplishments.

Leader: We come as we are, with strengths and weaknesses, each a child of God.

People: As we gather together this day let us open our hearts before the Lord.

Leader: And let us worship and give praise to God, Creator of all the world.

All: Blessed be the name of the Lord!

Collect

O God, You are the Almighty One, yet Your ear is always there for every prayer we whisper in the stillness of our hearts. You are so gracious and loving, help us to share everything with You. In Christ we pray. Amen.

Prayer Of Confession

Lord, so many times we live our lives as though we are all alone and without Your love. We often struggle to do what we do only by our own efforts. We often think and feel that we can take care of ourselves, and we fail to see Your sustaining presence in our lives. Forgive us, Lord, and help us accept Your love and Your help. In Christ we pray. Amen.

Hymns

"Sweet Hour Of Prayer"
"What A Friend We Have In Jesus"
"An Evening Prayer"

Proper 13
Sunday between July 31 and August 6 inclusive

First Lesson: Hosea 11:1-11
Theme: Justice tempered with compassion

Call To Worship

Leader: Praise be to the Lord God Almighty for our wonderful salvation!

People: Even when we were lost and wandering amid sin, the Lord sought us still.

Leader: We deserved God's terrible wrath, yet we received God's loving discipline.

People: As a parent guides a child, so has the Lord watched over our paths.

Leader: Let our witness to God's justice and compassion be clear.

All: Blessed be the name of the Lord!

Collect

O God, we have each one fallen so very short of what You created us to be, yet You have always guided us back into the ways You would have us go. We give You our praise and love, O Lord. In Christ we pray. Amen.

Prayer Of Confession

Lord, we often choose in our hearts to go our own ways in life without regard for the paths You would have us travel. We have even believed You would not care and there would be no price to pay. Forgive us, Lord, and draw us ever closer to You so that we might again share Your wonderful blessings with all we meet. In Christ we pray. Amen.

Hymns

"Without Him"
"Love Lifted Me"
"He Leadeth Me"

Proper 13
Sunday between July 31 and August 6 inclusive

Second Lesson: Colossians 3:1-11
Theme: Seeking the Kingdom of God

Call To Worship

Leader: Let all whose hearts are seeking the ways of Christ come now for worship!

People: We have tried the ways of the world, but in them we had no joy.

Leader: But in the ways of Christ we have the wonderful joy of salvation.

People: Then let us focus our lives on the things of God's kingdom.

Leader: And let us celebrate the eternity we receive through Christ our Savior!

All: Blessed be the name of the Lord!

Collect

O God, You have called us to see through Your eyes what is important in life, and in Christ You give us the love we need to live as citizens of Your kingdom. We praise You, O Lord. In Christ we pray. Amen.

Prayer Of Confession

Lord, even though You showed us through the cross and the resurrection that all You taught us was true and we must truly give up our lives to save them, we have still sought to find our security in the things of the material world. Forgive us, Lord, and help us keep our lives focused on living according to the things of Your kingdom. In Christ we pray. Amen.

Hymns

"Since Jesus Came Into My Heart"
"Seek Ye First"
"O To Be Like Thee"

Proper 13
Sunday between July 31 and August 6 inclusive

Gospel: Luke 12:13-21
Theme: Where are our treasures?

Call To Worship
Leader: Let all who love the Lord gather together in worship and praise.

People: But so much of the world today is focused on greed and destruction.

Leader: Yet we are called to share with the world God's redeeming love.

People: What must we do that all might know of God's mercy and grace?

Leader: Let us lift our voices in unison, proclaiming Christ for all to hear.

All: Blessed be the name of the Lord!

Collect
Most loving and just God, You call us to move beyond the values of the world and to store our treasures in You and eternity. Give us the courage to believe and to follow You, Lord. In Christ we pray. Amen.

Prayer Of Confession
Lord, so often we tend to drift toward the values of the world and away from the eternal values You came to teach us. So many times, Lord, we have chosen wealth and the worldly things over loving You or loving one another. Forgive us, Lord, and help us to keep our hearts turned toward the cross so the world might truly know Your love is real. In Christ we pray. Amen.

Hymns
"Jesu, Jesu"
"We've A Story To Tell To The Nations"
"Close To Thee"

150

Proper 14
Sunday between August 7 and August 13 inclusive

First Lesson: Isaiah 1:1, 10-20
Theme: Compassion not sacrifice

Call To Worship

Leader: Let us gather together this day and bring worship and praise to the Lord.

People: What may we bring, or what sacrifice can we make before Almighty God?

Leader: Let us bring the love in our hearts and our caring for our neighbors.

People: And let us seek justice in the world for all who are not powerful or rich.

Leader: God loves a cheerful heart, so let us celebrate in song and praise!

All: Blessed be the name of the Lord!

Collect

Almighty and loving God, in Your wonderful mercy and grace You have called us to carry Your love into the world, reach out to the poor, and seek justice for all. We praise You, O Lord. In Christ we pray. Amen.

Prayer Of Confession

Lord, we often have taken for granted Your mercy and grace, and we have not sought to extend Your gifts to others. Many times we have settled for seeking our own comfort and left the battle for justice in the world up to others. Forgive us, Lord, and open our eyes to the injustices around us so that we might get involved and truly make a difference. In Christ we pray. Amen.

Hymns

"Take Time To Be Holy"
"Jesus Loves Even Me"
"Onward, Christian Soldiers"

Proper 14
Sunday between August 7 and August 13 inclusive

Second Lesson: Hebrews 11:1-3, 8-16
Theme: Citizens by faith

Call To Worship
Leader: Let all who trust in Christ as their Lord and Savior come now for worship.
People: In things large and small we trust Christ in all that we do in life.
Leader: Faithful and true are the qualities shared by those in the Kingdom of God.
People: We can believe in no other because there is only one true living God.
Leader: Let our hearts be glad, for God calls us heirs in Christ our Savior.
All: Blessed be the name of the Lord!

Collect
Most gracious and loving God, even among the ancient ones You counted the faithful among Your children. Touch our hearts, Lord, and give us the wisdom, courage, and strength to be faithful. In Christ we pray. Amen.

Prayer Of Confession
Lord, so often we have let ourselves believe that it is the good things we have done rather than our faithful hearts that will earn our place in Your kingdom. We have even let ourselves entertain thoughts of our actually being worthy to be called Your children. Forgive us, Lord, and let us always be Your faithful and obedient servants. In Christ we pray. Amen.

Hymns
"My Faith Looks Up To Thee"
"At The Cross"
"Have Faith In God"

Proper 14
Sunday between August 7 and August 13 inclusive

Gospel: Luke 12:32-40
Theme: Be faithfully on watch

Call To Worship
Leader: Let all who love and worship the Lord come together!
People: Let us gather together in the security of God's house.
Leader: Let us rest in the safety of God's loving arms.
People: We pause together to worship amid the storms of life outside.
Leader: Then let us give praise to God this day for our eternal safety.
All: Blessed be the name of the Lord!

Collect
Almighty God, Lord of all, give us the strength to keep our focus on You and not to let the noise of the world around us detract us from being prepared for Your return. In Christ we pray. Amen.

Prayer Of Confession
Lord, we often allow our lives to be overshadowed by the problems and fears of the world, and we live in despair rather than accept Your hope and love. We have often become voices of defeat rather than living witnesses to Your victory on the cross. Forgive us, Lord, and give us faith that we might lead others to You. In Christ we pray. Amen.

Hymns
"Victory In Jesus"
"When The Roll Is Called Up Yonder"
"When We All Get To Heaven"

Proper 15
Sunday between August 14 and August 20 inclusive

First Lesson: Isaiah 5:1-7
Theme: Vineyard of justice and righteousness

Call To Worship

Leader: Let our voices be lifted in song and praise before Christ our Lord.

People: For we are called to be the servants of the Lord and to seek justice for all.

Leader: We are called to serve the Lord in all we do in work or in play,

People: So that the world might see in us witness to the love of Christ our Lord,

Leader: Let our hearts be joined in praise as we gather now for worship.

All: Blessed be the name of the Lord!

Collect

Most loving and merciful God, You have called us to the task of being Your beacons of justice and righteousness amid a cold and uncaring world. Sustain us as we serve You, Lord. In Christ we pray. Amen.

Prayer Of Confession

Lord, so often we only look after ourselves, and we let everyone else struggle on their own. Too often, we have thought it too much trouble to "get involved" to battle the injustices in the world around us. Forgive us, Lord, and as we remember the price You paid for us, let us be willing to give our lives for others. In Christ we pray. Amen.

Hymns

"Marching To Zion"
"He Keeps Me Singing"
"Peace, Be Still"

Proper 15
Sunday between August 14 and August 20 inclusive

Second Lesson: Hebrews 11:29—12:2
Theme: Faithfully fixing our eyes upon Jesus

Call To Worship

Leader: Come, let those who seek to serve Christ enter this place of worship!

People: We seek to serve Christ in all we do and say as we live every day.

Leader: Let our focus always be on Christ so our hearts will be filled with love.

People: Only in the love of Christ can we truly serve as we are called to do.

Leader: Not in our own power but in the Holy Name of Christ our Lord do we serve.

All: Blessed be the name of the Lord!

Collect

Most loving and merciful God, in Your infinite wisdom You allow us to serve in Your kingdom most effectively as we keep our focus upon Christ. We thank You, Lord, and give You our praise. In Christ we pray. Amen.

Prayer Of Confession

Lord, in our pride we have tried to serve You in our own wisdom and knowledge, and we have refused to seek and follow Your will. Too often, we have felt the matters of our everyday lives were not important enough to "bother" You about. Forgive us, Lord, and help us to remember everything we do every day witnesses to others of Your Lordship in our lives. In Christ we pray. Amen.

Hymns

"Turn Your Eyes Upon Jesus"
"Make Me A Blessing"
"Softly And Tenderly"

Proper 15
Sunday between August 14 and August 20 inclusive

Gospel: Luke 12:49-56
Theme: Standing true for Christ

Call To Worship

Leader: The peace of our Lord Jesus Christ be with you.

People: And the peace of the Lord be with you also.

Leader: Let the world see witnesses of God's grace through our lives.

People: Let us each one take courage and share the Gospel in all we do.

Leader: Even when the world will not hear, let us hold true and praise God.

All: Blessed be the name of the Lord!

Collect

O Lord, You called us to stand firm in our faith, even if the world, our friends, and our families do not understand. Give us the courage to be true and to seek only to serve You faithfully. In Christ we pray. Amen.

Prayer Of Confession

Lord, we often seek the approval of the world and lose sight of the message You would have our lives bring to those around us. Or we have feared rejection and not seen how Your rejection on the cross brought healing and love. Forgive us, Lord, when we have lost our way, and lead us so that our lives might lead others to You. In Christ we pray. Amen.

Hymns

"I Know Whom I Have Believed"
"Wonderful Words Of Life"
"Seek Ye First"

Proper 16
Sunday between August 21 and August 27 inclusive

First Lesson: Jeremiah 1:4-10
Theme: Messengers of God

Call To Worship

Leader: Let all who would proclaim the Good News of Christ enter now for worship.

People: In Christ we have life and salvation. Let us proclaim the Gospel of Christ.

Leader: We are called to be God's messengers in the world around us today.

People: If we who have received salvation will not declare it, then who will?

Leader: Truly those who have heard the Word of the Lord are God's messengers.

All: Blessed be the name of the Lord!

Collect

O God, we are so grateful for the salvation You gave us through Christ, and we hear Your call that we should spread the Good News. Give us the words to say and the wisdom to use them. In Christ we pray. Amen.

Prayer Of Confession

Lord, we often allow ourselves to be led astray into the concerns of the world and we forget our call to share the Gospel of Christ. Too often, we have been more concerned about what our next meal will be or how we will make the next car payment than we have been about telling others about Your redeeming love. Forgive us, Lord. In Christ we pray. Amen.

Hymns

"I Love To Tell The Story"
"O For A Thousand Tongues To Sing"
"My Redeemer"

157

Proper 16
Sunday between August 21 and August 27 inclusive

Second Lesson: Hebrews 12:18-29
Theme: The unshakable Kingdom of God

Call To Worship
Leader: The Lord our God is the Alpha and the Omega and shall be Lord forever!

People: No matter what the problems in our lives, God is still our Creator God.

Leader: The earth may tremble and the storms may blow, but no power can equal God.

People: Let our faith and hope rest in the Lord Who does not change or fail us.

Leader: Truly the Lord our God is wonderful and greatly to be praised.

All: Blessed be the name of the Lord!

Collect
Almighty Creator God, You and You alone hold and sustain the entire Universe in Your loving hands and no force can endure against Your Kingdom, yet You love us still. We praise You, O God. In Christ we pray. Amen.

Prayer Of Confession
O God, even though we know You are our Creator and Sustainer and that Your Kingdom will be victorious for all eternity, so often we have yielded to the worldly pressures to believe our only hope lives in our worldly wisdom and science. Forgive us, Lord, and help us to remember that it is You we serve in this hurting and need-filled world. In Christ we pray. Amen.

Hymns
"O Jesus, I Have Promised"
"Others"
"This Is My Father's World"

Proper 16
Sunday between August 21 and August 27 inclusive

Gospel: Luke 13:10-17
Theme: Love is greater than the Law

Call To Worship
Leader: Let all who would know the freedom of God's grace come together!

People: Must we know all the Laws and must we be perfect in our hearts?

Leader: Jesus fulfilled the Law, and in Christ we are perfected before God.

People: What if our clothes are not fine or our bodies imperfect and worn?

Leader: Sing praises unto the Lord! In the cross, God's love came to us all!

All: Blessed be the name of the Lord!

Collect
Most loving and merciful God, You saw that we were bound and hurting under the laws that were meant to lead us to You, and in Christ You sent us Your healing love. Lord, we give You our praise. In Christ we pray. Amen.

Prayer Of Confession
Lord, we have placed what we see as "right" above the patience and understanding that You would have us bring to the world. In our pride, we have lived "by the rules" as we spread hatred and division toward those who we feel fall short of Your standards. Forgive us, Lord, and help us remember the mercy You freely gave to us. In Christ we pray. Amen.

Hymns
"Love Divine, All Loves Excelling"
"Because He Lives"
"Love Lifted Me"

159

Proper 17
Sunday between August 28 and September 3 inclusive

First Lesson: Jeremiah 2:4-13
Theme: Iniquities of the unfaithful

Call To Worship

Leader: Joyful people, come and let us worship Christ our Lord and Savior!

People: For we were once in darkness, and the Lord called us to salvation.

Leader: But we are given God's blessing of salvation so that we might serve Christ.

People: We are called to serve the Lord by caring and loving those around us.

Leader: Then let us share the joy of the Lord with all who will receive it.

All: Blessed be the name of the Lord!

Collect

Almighty God, in Your mercy and grace You have not forsaken us even when we do not fight for the justice and righteousness for which You called us. We thank You, O Lord. In Christ we pray. Amen.

Prayer Of Confession

Lord, so often we have not defended the poor or fed the hungry, instead we have focused on making our lives more comfortable. Lord, we have even allowed ourselves to think that if we are doing well the world is "just fine." Forgive us, Lord, and call us again to do battle against the inequities and injustices in the world today. In Christ we pray. Amen.

Hymns

"Pass It On"
"Take The Name Of Jesus With You"
"Jesus Calls Us"

Proper 17
Sunday between August 28 and September 3 inclusive

Second Lesson: Hebrews 13:1-8, 15-16
Theme: Duties in Christ's love

Call To Worship

Leader: Let all who seek to serve the Lord with gladness come now for worship!

People: We serve the Lord with joyful hearts, for Christ touches others through us.

Leader: Seeing the Lord touch and restore others confirms our joy and faith.

People: Then let us be about the tasks Christ has called us to do.

Leader: And let our songs and praise ring out for all the world to hear!

All: Blessed be the name of the Lord!

Collect

O Lord, in Your wonderful way You have called us to be about the work of Your Kingdom so that we might receive the gift of life that You offer to us. We thank You and give You our praise. In Christ we pray. Amen.

Prayer Of Confession

Lord, too often we have not clearly understood the harm we may do or the gifts and blessings we may miss when we are not faithful in conducting our lives in the loving way You called us to live. We have not seen the negative reactions we caused toward You, Lord, when we acted rudely or in uncaring ways toward others. Forgive us, Lord. In Christ we pray. Amen.

Hymns

"Moment By Moment"
"He Touched Me"
"Reach Out And Touch"

161

Proper 17
Sunday between August 28 and September 3 inclusive

Gospel: Luke 14:1, 7-14
Theme: Humble servants of the Lord

Call To Worship

Leader: Let all who love the Lord gather in this house and worship.

People: Let the great and the small and the rich and the poor come.

Leader: Let the mighty and the weak and the proud and the humble come.

People: Let our hearts be focused this day on the glory of the Lord.

Leader: Let us sing with joy that we are all made welcome in God's house.

All: Blessed be the name of the Lord!

Collect

Almighty Creator God, in Christ You called us to be humble and to take up our crosses and follow You. Give us the wisdom and strength to hear Your call and be Your faithful followers. In Christ we pray. Amen.

Prayer Of Confession

Lord, You taught us not to be puffed up or full of pride, yet so often we seek our own glory. You lived Your life in true humility, yet so often we seek prideful greatness. Lord, You offer us Your loving forgiveness, yet so often we will not forgive others. Forgive us again and heal our hearts, Lord, and help us share Your love with others. In Christ we pray. Amen.

Hymns

"Take My Life And Let It Be"
"Here I Am, Lord"
"Take Time To Be Holy"

162

Proper 18
Sunday between September 4 and September 10 inclusive

First Lesson: Jeremiah 18:1-11
Theme: Clay in the Potter's hands

Call To Worship
Leader: Let all who seek to grow in their faith enter this place for worship!

People: We would have the Lord mold us and shape us into God's people today.

Leader: God is the Potter and we are the clay in the Great Creator's hands.

People: We yield our lives unto the Lord to mold us as is pleasing before God.

Leader: Praise be to the Lord, for God is faithful to prepare us for eternity.

All: Blessed be the name of the Lord!

Collect
Most loving and merciful God, in Your wisdom You take even the tragedies in our lives and use them to make of us better people. Help us, Lord, to entrust ever more of our lives to You. In Christ we pray. Amen.

Prayer Of Confession
Lord, like children we insist that we can manage by ourselves, and we have tried to deny You the opportunity to guide us and lead us into becoming the mature people of faith You created us to be. We have missed both receiving Your blessings and being able to pass them on to others because of our stubbornness. Forgive us, Lord. In Christ we pray. Amen.

Hymns
"Have Thine Own Way, Lord"
"Where He Leads Me"
"Trust And Obey"

Proper 18
Sunday between September 4 and September 10 inclusive

Second Lesson: Philemon 1-21
Theme: The Christian bond

Call To Worship

Leader: Come, let all who love Christ gather for worship this day!
People: In Christ we are made one family, sisters and brothers before God.
Leader: Christ renews our spirits and cleanses our souls of sin.
People: Indeed, in Christ we are made new, no longer bound by sin's powers.
Leader: Let us praise the Lord for the bond we share through the work of Christ.
All: Blessed be the name of the Lord!

Collect

O God, even before we knew our sins through Christ You opened the way for our salvation so that we might be made new again. Help us, Lord, to love each other as You first loved us. In Christ we pray. Amen.

Prayer Of Confession

Lord, so often we have failed to realize that special bond You intended us to share as Your precious children. We have been unduly critical and judgmental of new Christians instead of guiding and nurturing them as they grow in their faith. Forgive us, Lord, and fill us anew with Your love so that we might share it again with others. In Christ we pray. Amen.

Hymns

"Lord, I Want To Be A Christian"
"Blest Be The Tie That Binds"
"I Am Thine, O Lord"

Proper 18
Sunday between September 4 and September 10 inclusive

Gospel: Luke 14:25-33
Theme: Counting the cost

Call To Worship
Leader: Let all who seek the Lord gather together in this house of worship.
People: **Let our hearts remember the cross and all that it calls us to be.**
Leader: Let us see in the cross the price paid so that we might know God's love.
People: **Let us walk then without fear, and be willing to accept our crosses.**
Leader: Let us give thanks to the Lord for we are redeemed children of God.
All: **Blessed be the name of the Lord!**

Collect
Most loving and merciful God, in the cross Your absolute love for us was made very clear, and we hear anew Your call for us to take up our crosses and follow. Help us to endure, Lord. In Christ we pray. Amen.

Prayer Of Confession
Lord, so often we desire to be a part of Your family, but we are unwilling to accept our crosses. We would be called Christians, but we are not always willing to live as You taught us. We would be Your followers, but so often we shrink away when faced with the price we might be called to pay. Forgive us, Lord, and give us courage to live for You. In Christ we pray. Amen.

Hymns
"Where He Leads Me"
"O Jesus, I Have Promised"
"Living For Jesus"

165

Proper 19
Sunday between September 11 and September 17 inclusive

First Lesson: Jeremiah 4:11-12, 22-28
Theme: Accountable to God

Call To Worship

Leader: Praise be to the Lord, who has set us free from sin and death!

People: Even while we were lost in our sin, Christ died that we might have life.

Leader: But we are saved that we might serve the Lord through all of our days;

People: Bound by our love and gratitude for God's redeeming love in Christ.

Leader: God remembers those who are faithful, so let us give voice to our praise.

All: Blessed be the name of the Lord!

Collect

Almighty and gracious God, in Your mercy You have again and again led Your children to repent from our sins. Help us to remain faithful, Lord, seeking only Your will in our lives. In Christ we pray. Amen.

Prayer Of Confession

Lord, in our pride we have often turned away from You into sin until You finally allowed us to face the consequences of our choices. Even when You have sent us word, calling us to repent so that You might spare us from judgment, we would not listen. Forgive us, Lord, and give us the ears to hear Your word and the faith to repent of our sins. In Christ we pray. Amen.

Hymns

"Only Trust Him"
"I Have Decided To Follow Jesus"
"Fill My Cup, Lord"

Proper 19
Sunday between September 11 and September 17 inclusive

Second Lesson: 1 Timothy 1:12-17
Theme: Grace beyond sin

Call To Worship

Leader: Let all who have known the grace and mercy of the Lord give praise!

People: For we were once so lost in our sin that we could not believe in God's grace.

Leader: Yet God's love for us is greater than all the sin in the world.

People: And all who accept Christ know that God's grace and forgiveness are real!

Leader: Let us rejoice and give praise for the redeeming love of Christ.

All: Blessed be the name of the Lord!

Collect

O God, in Christ You opened the way for us to receive Your restoring grace if we will only repent and live for You. Give us the courage to entrust all we are or ever will be to You, Lord. In Christ we pray. Amen.

Prayer Of Confession

O God, we have often been quick to judge others, and we have failed to remember that we have been redeemed only by Your mercy and grace. Somehow the sins of others seem more worthy of judgment than our own, and too often we have chosen to judge for ourselves. Forgive us, Lord, and help us to remember that the grace we have received is abundant enough for all. In Christ we pray. Amen.

Hymns

"Grace Greater Than Our Sin"
"God Of Grace And God Of Glory"
"Amazing Grace"

Proper 19
Sunday between September 11 and September 17 inclusive

Gospel: Luke 15:1-10
Theme: Seeking the lost

Call To Worship

Leader: Let all who love the Lord enter this place and worship!

People: But we are sinners, unclean and unworthy to be in the house of God.

Leader: In Christ, God's grace became full, and we are made welcome to enter.

People: Then let us enter that we may tell all the nations of God's mercy.

Leader: Come! Worship! Sing praises unto our Almighty Loving God!

All: Blessed be the name of the Lord!

Collect

Almighty Creator God, You are indeed our Good Shepherd, and we are so blessed to be a part of Your flock. Give us the loving heart to seek others who are lost and bring them to You. In Christ we pray. Amen.

Prayer Of Confession

Lord, so often we have received Your love but have not understood it. You have forgiven us, but we have not seen our need to forgive others. You have shown us mercy, but we have not in turn been merciful to others. You have granted us Your grace, but we have not extended grace around us. Forgive us, Lord, and open our hearts to Your love. In Christ we pray. Amen.

Hymns

"Rescue The Perishing"
"We've A Story To Tell To The Nations"
"Pass It On"

Proper 20
Sunday between September 18 and September 24 inclusive

First Lesson: Jeremiah 8:18—9:1
Theme: The agony of God

Call To Worship

Leader: Come, let us celebrate God's wonderful redeeming love!

People: For even while we were yet in sin God loved us and felt our pain.

Leader: God's sorrows over our sins are real and the Lord sees the love we miss.

People: God has many blessings for all who repent, but sin must be judged.

Leader: Then let us repent and seek the Lord with praise and joyful worship.

All: Blessed be the name of the Lord!

Collect

Most wonderful and loving God, like a parent You have watched over us and felt the pain and agony of our sins and mistakes. Give us the courage, Lord, to seek Your loving guidance. In Christ we pray. Amen.

Prayer Of Confession

Lord, like stubborn and willful children we have each one turned from You to seek our own way in life. As earthly parents we feel the agony in our hearts when children we love turn away and hurt us, but we are slow to realize that in our pride and self-determination we have also rejected You. Forgive us, O Lord, and call us again to be Your children. In Christ we pray. Amen.

Hymns

"Must Jesus Bear The Cross Alone"
"At The Cross"
"No, Not One"

169

Proper 20
Sunday between September 18 and September 24 inclusive

Second Lesson: 1 Timothy 2:1-7
Theme: Christ our mediator

Call To Worship

Leader: Let our hearts be filled with praise and thanksgiving before the Lord!

People: But we are not worthy to stand before Almighty God, Creator of the Universe.

Leader: Yes, but Christ is our mediator and stands before God to plead our case.

People: In Christ are we found worthy and made welcome before God's throne?

Leader: In Christ we are washed clean of our sins and found righteous before God.

All: Blessed be the name of the Lord!

Collect

Most loving God, in Your infinite wisdom You knew we could never stand before You righteous and free from sin, yet You loved us enough to redeem us in Christ. We praise You, Lord. In Christ we pray. Amen.

Prayer Of Confession

Lord, in our pride and arrogance we have felt ourselves worthy to be in Your presence and deserving of Your mercy and grace. Too often we have been totally unaware of the sin in our lives, much less aware of how unrighteous we were in Your eyes. Forgive us, Lord, and help us remember we are redeemed only by Your mercy, love, and grace. In Christ we pray. Amen.

Hymns

"What A Friend We Have In Jesus"
"Standing On The Promises"
"Through It All"

Proper 20
Sunday between September 18 and September 24 inclusive

Gospel: Luke 16:1-13
Theme: Which Master will we serve?

Call To Worship

Leader: Come, all who are faithful, and let us worship the Lord God Almighty!

People: But the world around us has turned away from God's mercy and grace.

Leader: Then we must give witness together of God's truth and righteousness.

People: Yet the world mocks and ridicules us, trying to silence our voices.

Leader: Then proclaim all the louder the certainty of God's victory to come.

All: Blessed be the name of the Lord!

Collect

Most loving Lord, You know the world sets before Your sheep strong and powerful temptations. Give us the wisdom to serve only You, O Lord, and the ears to hear Your guidance. In Christ we pray. Amen.

Prayer Of Confession

O God, Creator and Sustainer of the Universe, so many times we let the people and circumstances that surround us cloud our vision and dull our spirits. Too often, when faced with difficult times, we panic and forget You are God. Strengthen and guide us, Lord, that we might become beacons of hope to the hurting world in which we live. In Christ we pray. Amen.

Hymns

"O Jesus, I Have Promised"
"Lord, I Want To Be A Christian"
"Close To Thee"

Proper 21
Sunday between September 25 and October 1 inclusive

First Lesson: Jeremiah 32:1-3a, 6-15
Theme: Faith beyond adversity

Call To Worship

Leader: Let us give praise to the Lord and celebrate God's love in our lives!

People: But times have been hard and the way in life has not seemed a blessing.

Leader: Yet the Lord is faithful and with us no matter what the circumstances.

People: Are we to celebrate the love of God even in the depths of life's crises?

Leader: Let us celebrate God's love, for the hard times will not last forever.

All: Blessed be the name of the Lord!

Collect

Most gracious and loving God, You have given us permission to celebrate even in the midst of adversity, for history and eternity belong to You. We give You our praise and thanksgiving, Lord. In Christ we pray. Amen.

Prayer Of Confession

Lord, when faced with even the slightest of difficulties in life, we have been quick to give up our faith or even to doubt that You are indeed God. In our worst times, Lord, we have allowed ourselves to chase after other powers, seeking answers for the problems we do not understand rather than calling upon Your guidance in faith. Forgive us, Lord. In Christ we pray. Amen.

Hymns

"Stand By Me"
"Precious Lord, Take My Hand"
"O Master, Let Me Walk With Thee"

Proper 21
Sunday between September 25 and October 1 inclusive

Second Lesson: 1 Timothy 6:6-19
Theme: Contentment in Christ

Call To Worship

Leader: Let us lift up our praise for the wonderful blessings of the Lord!

People: But many among the faithful are not rich nor do they have nice clothes.

Leader: Yet if we have food and cover for this day, we have what is needed.

People: But the standards of the world and our hearts are greater than this.

Leader: The world does not hold eternity, and Christ had not even a place to stay.

All: Blessed be the name of the Lord!

Collect

Almighty and loving God, in Christ You showed us that contentment is not built on the things of this world. Give us the courage and strength, Lord, to seek Your standards and not the world's. In Christ we pray. Amen.

Prayer Of Confession

Lord, so often we have forsaken all You came to teach us, and we have dedicated most of our lives to obtaining and possessing things that will not be treasures laid up in heaven. Forgive us, Lord, and help us to realize that seeking after the wants of our hearts, unless they are submitted to Your standards, will not lead us into eternity with You. In Christ we pray. Amen.

Hymns

"Oh, To Be Like Thee"
"His Eye Is On The Sparrow"
"I Surrender All"

Proper 21
Sunday between September 25 and October 1 inclusive

Gospel: Luke 16:19-31
Theme: Service yields eternal rewards

Call To Worship

Leader: Let all who would follow Christ gather in worship and praise.

People: Let our hearts sing praises to God for all of the ways we are blessed.

Leader: Yet let us also see and hear those in need around us, and let us help.

People: For we are not called just to seek and receive blessings from God,

Leader: But to be God's blessings to all in need of a healing word today.

All: Blessed be the name of the Lord!

Collect

O righteous and merciful God, You have called us to service and warned us of the consequences should we choose the ways of the world instead. Call us anew to walk only with You. In Christ we pray. Amen.

Prayer Of Confession

Lord, too often we get so involved with our own special interests in life that we become blind to those around us who are hurting and in need. Too often our goals are high and lofty, yet we fail to see the hungry sitting right at our feet. Forgive us, Lord, and open our hearts to Your vision of those in need here and around the world. In Christ we pray. Amen.

Hymns

"When We Walk With The Lord"
"I Am Thine, O Lord"
"Jesu, Jesu"

174

Proper 22
Sunday between October 2 and October 8 inclusive

First Lesson: Lamentations 1:1-6
Theme: The agony of sin

Call To Worship

Leader: Gather now for worship, all who would seek to be faithful to the Lord!

People: The Lord is our salvation and in no other name can we know genuine life.

Leader: For the wages of sin are truly death, both to our spirit and to our body.

People: In sin we knew desolation, for the Spirit of the Lord was not with us.

Leader: But in Christ we are redeemed and the Spirit of the Lord gives us life.

All: Blessed be the name of the Lord!

Collect

Most wonderful God, in Your mercy and grace You have allowed us to experience a taste of the price we must pay for sin. Lord, give us the wisdom and strength to be faithful servants. In Christ we pray. Amen.

Prayer Of Confession

Lord, so often as we have experienced the emptiness of sinful life we have become bitter and hateful instead of repenting and returning to You. Too often, Lord, we have even vented our anger and shown our resentment over the discomfort we feel by seeking after our own gods. Forgive us, Lord, and lead us again to a life of faith and repentance. In Christ we pray. Amen.

Hymns

"All Your Anxiety"
"Higher Ground"
"Revive Us Again"

Proper 22
Sunday between October 2 and October 8 inclusive

Second Lesson: 2 Timothy 1:1-14
Theme: Bold and confident faith

Call To Worship
Leader: Let all who proclaim Jesus Christ as their Lord come now for worship!

People: We are children of the living God, adopted through the cross of Christ.

Leader: Let us proclaim the mighty power of Christ for all the world to hear.

People: The love of Christ has touched our souls and redeemed us before God.

Leader: Let us lift our praise to the Lord, whose love gives us life eternal.

All: Blessed be the name of the Lord!

Collect
O God, in Christ You have given us life eternal and joy in our hearts no matter what the circumstances in life that surround us. Help us to proclaim the wonder of Your love in all the world. In Christ we pray. Amen.

Prayer Of Confession
Lord, so often when we could have boldly declared what Your love has meant in our lives we have instead been timid or even silent. When we could have shared Your Good News with a personal word of faith to a hurting world, we have instead chosen to speak in meaningless platitudes. Forgive us, Lord, and once again call us to proclaim Your Gospel. In Christ we pray. Amen.

Hymns
"There Shall Be Showers Of Blessings"
"I Am Thine, O Lord"
"My Jesus, I Love Thee"

Proper 22
Sunday between October 2 and October 8 inclusive

Gospel: Luke 17:5-10
Theme: The power of faith

Call To Worship

Leader: Let us gather together and declare our faith for all to hear.

People: But our faith is small and our witness seems so weak.

Leader: The Lord has promised to do great works with only the tiniest faith.

People: But dare we trust and truly step out; will the Lord honor our faith?

Leader: Step out on your faith! The Lord is faithful to all who will obey.

All: Blessed be the name of the Lord!

Collect

Most loving and gracious Lord, in Your infinite wisdom You have called us to be people of faith who can move the mountains of life. Increase our faith, Lord, that we may serve others. In Christ we pray. Amen.

Prayer Of Confession

Lord, sometimes we are so timid. Even when we hear Your word clearly, we will not trust and follow. Your ways are not the world's ways and too often we would seek the security we think we see in the world. Forgive us, Lord, and help us learn how to use the grain of faith You have given us so that we might move the mountains in life. In Christ we pray. Amen.

Hymns

"Have Faith In God"
"How Firm A Foundation"
"Hymn Of Promise"

Proper 23
Sunday between October 9 and October 15 inclusive

First Lesson: Jeremiah 29:1, 4-7
Theme: Faithfully witness wherever we are

Call To Worship

Leader: Let us proclaim the glory of the Lord in our praise and worship!

People: And let our lives bear witness to God's salvation in Christ.

Leader: For the Lord is with us always, in good times or in hard times.

People: And wherever we are we can give witness to our loving God.

Leader: Let our voices be lifted in praise and song for God's wonderful love.

All: Blessed be the name of the Lord!

Collect

Most wonderful and loving God, in Your infinite mercy and grace You have remained with us and loved us, even when we have suffered the consequences of our sins. We praise You, O Lord. In Christ we pray. Amen.

Prayer Of Confession

Lord, when times have not been comfortable for us we have turned away from You or questioned how You could allow hard times to befall us. We have even been so concerned about our own needs that we have failed to see the openings before us to share Your Good News with those who need the peace and hope Your Gospel can bring. Forgive us, Lord. In Christ we pray. Amen.

Hymns

"Jesu, Jesu"
"I Want A Principle Within"
"I Will Sing Of My Redeemer"

178

Proper 23
Sunday between October 9 and October 15 inclusive

Second Lesson: 2 Timothy 2:8-15
Theme: Unashamed laborers for Christ

Call To Worship

Leader: Let us boldly proclaim the Good News of Christ throughout the world!

People: Wherever we go let our voices give praise to the Lord for our salvation.

Leader: And let us not be ashamed to offer Christ to those who know us well.

People: For we have been made new and our sins and transgressions are forgiven.

Leader: In Christ we have life and we have it beyond all measure or limit.

All: Blessed be the name of the Lord!

Collect

Most loving and merciful Lord, You have given us Your love and the hope of eternity, and You ask in return only that we spread Your Good News. Lord, help us share Your Gospel effectively. In Christ we pray. Amen.

Prayer Of Confession

Lord, too often in our lives we have allowed the opinions of others to be more important to us than being faithful to You. Somehow, Lord, we allow ourselves to fear the rejection of our "friends" if we try to share Your Gospel more than we fear Your eternal rejection if we do not share Christ. Forgive us, Lord, and help us share Your Gospel boldly. In Christ we pray. Amen.

Hymns

"Bringing In The Sheaves"
"I Have Decided To Follow Jesus"
"In Christ There Is No East Or West"

179

Proper 23
Sunday between October 9 and October 15 inclusive

Gospel: Luke 17:11-19
Theme: The grateful and the ungrateful

Call To Worship

Leader: Let our hearts sound forth with praise for the mercy of the Lord!

People: In Christ we are forgiven and in Christ we are made righteous.

Leader: Then let us proclaim the good news for all the world to hear!

People: And let us reach out, even to our neighbor, with God's healing love.

Leader: For God sent the Christ, that we should have everlasting hope.

All: Blessed be the name of the Lord!

Collect

O God, Creator of the Universe, in Your mercy and grace You have chosen to touch our lives and bless us. Help us share Your blessings so that others might come to love and serve You. In Christ we pray. Amen.

Prayer Of Confession

Lord, so many times You have granted our prayers only to see us happily go our way without even a word of thanks. So often when a word of praise for Your mercy and grace in our lives might have led others to know and trust You, we have been silent instead. Forgive us, Lord, and help us to proclaim boldly Your love for all to hear. In Christ we pray. Amen.

Hymns

"Count Your Blessings"
"Jesus, We Just Want To Thank You"
"This Is My Father's World"

Proper 24
Sunday between October 16 and October 22 inclusive

First Lesson: Jeremiah 31:27-34
Theme: Promise of the New Covenant

Call To Worship

Leader: Let us gather for worship and praise before Almighty God!

People: We come before the Lord through the salvation of the New Covenant.

Leader: The New Covenant was promised in the ancient days and delivered by Christ.

People: The New Covenant draws us together under the cleansing blood of Christ.

Leader: Let us celebrate the New Covenant, always giving God our joyful praise.

All: Blessed be the name of the Lord!

Collect

Most loving and gracious God, in Your infinite wisdom You saw our desperate need for a New Covenant to be written on our hearts. Help us to live and spread the New Covenant of Christ. In Christ we pray. Amen.

Prayer Of Confession

Lord, we have often taken for granted the gift You have given us in the New Covenant. Even if our lives have been changed through Your wonderful restoring word, we have often remained silent, failing to let others know how they also might experience Your love and restoration. Forgive us, Lord, and help us proclaim the Good News of Christ. In Christ we pray. Amen.

Hymns

"Leaning On The Everlasting Arms"
"On Christ The Solid Rock I Stand"
"Trust And Obey"

181

Proper 24
Sunday between October 16 and October 22 inclusive

Second Lesson: 2 Timothy 3:14—4:5
Theme: Fulfilling our ministries

Call To Worship

Leader: Let us come together to worship and learn the ways of the Lord!

People: Let us study the scriptures, that we might hear God's Word in them.

Leader: Let us join together in prayer, that we might know God's presence.

People: Let us seek to walk with the Lord, that others might see God with us.

Leader: Let us sing out with joy and give praise for God's mercy and love!

All: Blessed be the name of the Lord!

Collect

O God, we would be true in our service to You. As we study the Scriptures and seek to know Your will in our lives, hear our prayers and give us the wisdom only You can provide. In Christ we pray. Amen.

Prayer Of Confession

Lord, so often we would study and know the Scriptures, but we are slow to allow You to change our hearts through them. Often we seek Your will for us and yet we do not have the courage to walk where You would have us walk. Forgive us, Lord, and help us hear afresh of Your mercy and love and share the Good News with all the world around us. In Christ we pray. Amen.

Hymns

"What Does The Lord Require"
"Jesus Saves"
"Send The Light"

Proper 24
Sunday between October 16 and October 22 inclusive

Gospel: Luke 18:1-8
Theme: God hears our prayers

Call To Worship

Leader: Let us enter the house of the Lord for a time of worship and praise!

People: And let our prayers be lifted up before the Lord God of Hosts.

Leader: Even the wishes of our hearts are heard before the throne of God.

People: Then let our worship be full of joy and gladness for God's loving care.

Leader: Let us carry to every people and land the news of Christ our Savior!

All: Blessed be the name of the Lord!

Collect

O God, we are so grateful that You opened the door through prayer for us to come to You with any matter that comes to our hearts. Help us to trust You, Lord, with every concern we have. In Christ we pray. Amen.

Prayer Of Confession

Lord, so often we have taken for granted the wonderful gift of prayer You have given us. We have not shared with You our burdens or we have not lifted up our loved ones or the needs of our church or the needs of the world around us. We have often ignored prayer or we have turned to it only when all else failed. Forgive us, Lord. In Christ we pray. Amen.

Hymns

"Near To The Heart Of God"
"Sweet Hour Of Prayer"
"Lord, Teach Us How To Pray Aright"

Proper 25
Sunday between October 23 and October 29 inclusive

First Lesson: Joel 2:23-32
Theme: Prophecy, dreams, and visions

Call To Worship

Leader: Let us gather this day to hear the wonderful word of the Lord!

People: For in God's Word we have salvation and the promise of God's eternity.

Leader: In the Kingdom of God the Spirit of the Lord will pour out its blessings.

People: And our young men and women will proclaim God's holy Word.

Leader: The dreams and visions of the generations will glorify God.

All: Blessed be the name of the Lord!

Collect

Most loving and gracious God, in Your infinite wisdom You gave us the prophecies of old which still fill our hearts with excitement. Pour out Your Spirit anew, Lord, and bless us again. In Christ we pray. Amen.

Prayer Of Confession

Lord, so often we have not sought to hear Your word nor have we been willing to accept Your messengers. Too often, Lord, we have wanted to hear only that part of Your word with which we were already comfortable. Forgive us, Lord, and open our hearts so we may hear all of Your Word, even if it calls us to task or comes from those different than we are. In Christ we pray. Amen.

Hymns

"Spirit Song"
"Open My Eyes"
"Here I Am, Lord"

Proper 25
Sunday between October 23 and October 29 inclusive

Second Lesson: 2 Timothy 4:6-8, 16-18
Theme: Finishing the race

Call To Worship
Leader: Let all who are committed to serving the Lord gather now for worship!
People: We will serve Christ our Lord with all we are and with all we have.
Leader: We must be faithful in our service all the days of our lives.
People: There is no other who is worthy but the Lord God Almighty.
Leader: Let our hearts be set on the prize that awaits all who are faithful.
All: Blessed be the name of the Lord!

Collect
Most wonderful and loving God, in Your mercy and grace You have called us to walk with You all the days of our lives. Help us to be faithful servants, Lord, until we see You face to face. In Christ we pray. Amen.

Prayer Of Confession
Lord, so often we have treated our faith as if it were something to be used only when we needed it, but when the way of Christ came between us and what we desired we felt we could simply set our faith on the shelf for a while. Forgive us, Lord, and help us to realize that our witness never ends and it will either be for You or it will not reflect Your love. In Christ we pray. Amen.

Hymns
"Saved By Grace"
"When The Roll Is Called Up Yonder"
"Until Then"

Proper 25
Sunday between October 23 and October 29 inclusive

Gospel: Luke 18:9-14
Theme: The trap of self-righteousness

Call To Worship

Leader: We gather in Your house, Lord, humbly and with prayerful hearts.

People: For each of us has gone astray in our own way before God.

Leader: Yet in Christ each of us is lovingly welcomed in God's house.

People: Then let us not judge each other; instead let us extend God's grace.

Leader: For in God's grace alone are we made clean, that none should boast.

All: Blessed be the name of the Lord!

Collect

O Lord, You did not seek Your heavenly glory, but instead set it aside so that we might know the nature of God's love. Help us to accept that we are righteous only in You; we dare not boast of self. In Christ we pray. Amen.

Prayer Of Confession

Lord, so often we compare our lives to others as we try to feel that we are better than they are, and we ignore the standard You set for us on the cross. Too often, like the Pharisees, our prayers are full of pride instead of the true humility that befits forgiven sinners. Forgive us, Lord, and help us celebrate Your grace by loving each other. In Christ we pray. Amen.

Hymns

"Be Thou My Vision"
"Have Thine Own Way, Lord"
"I Surrender All"

Proper 26
Sunday between October 30 and November 5 inclusive

First Lesson: Habakkuk 1:1-4; 2:1-4
Theme: Sin, judgment, and faith

Call To Worship

Leader: Come, let the people of God give praise and worship the Lord!

People: For we have sinned before the Lord, yet in Christ we have been forgiven.

Leader: God honors repentance and will not judge those who have turned from sin.

People: But what of those who have not repented and turned from their sin?

Leader: God will not be mocked nor can sin go on without receiving judgment.

All: Blessed be the name of the Lord!

Collect

Almighty and just Lord, in Your mercy and grace You have called us to repentance so that we might not experience the wages of sin. Give us the vision and the wisdom to follow Your leading, Lord. In Christ we pray. Amen.

Prayer Of Confession

Lord, we often act as if somehow we can continue to sin and turn away from Your will for our lives and still not experience Your judgment for our actions. We have even allowed ourselves to think that because we are called Christians You would never discipline us for our sins. Forgive us, Lord, and call us again to repentance. In Christ we pray. Amen.

Hymns

"Cleanse Me"
"Standing In The Need Of Prayer"
"Rock Of Ages"

Proper 26
Sunday between October 30 and November 5 inclusive

Second Lesson: 2 Thessalonians 1:1-4, 11-12
Theme: Living witnesses to God's power

Call To Worship

Leader: Gather now together for worship, all who would serve the risen Christ!

People: Christ is our salvation and worthy to be greatly praised.

Leader: Christ has touched the lives and souls of many, restoring their hope.

People: For in Christ we have the promise of eternity, so we fear not the world.

Leader: Let our living witness be filled with joyful praise and song unto God.

All: Blessed be the name of the Lord!

Collect

Most loving and merciful God, through Your grace You have called us to be living witnesses for the Good News of Christ in the world. Lord, as we are willing to serve, give us the words to say. In Christ we pray. Amen.

Prayer Of Confession

Lord, we have received the blessings of our salvation yet we have often been slow to be witnesses of God's redeeming love. We have even felt that the task of spreading the Gospel of Christ was best left up to the professionals. Forgive us, Lord, and help us to realize what powerful witnesses You intended us to be. In Christ we pray. Amen.

Hymns

"Standing On The Promises"
"A Charge To Keep I Have"
" 'Tis So Sweet To Trust In Jesus"

Proper 26
Sunday between October 30 and November 5 inclusive

Gospel: Luke 19:1-10
Theme: Serving the Lord; seeking the lost

Call To Worship

Leader: We come together today seeking the Lord in this house of worship.

People: We seek the Lord so that our lives might be touched and made whole.

Leader: We seek the Lord, for in Christ we see that God first sought us.

People: We seek the Lord, because it is in Christ that we have true life.

Leader: Let us sing and give praise to God for the Christ, who is our Savior!

All: Blessed be the name of the Lord!

Collect

O Lord, You so freely gave of Yourself that we might receive salvation. Help us, O Lord, to freely give of ourselves that others might come to know about and receive Your salvation. In Christ we pray. Amen.

Prayer Of Confession

Lord, we often chase after the things of the world, thinking they will give us peace, joy, and life, instead of seeking Your will for us. Too often we have let the opinions of others be more important to us than Your Word. Forgive us, Lord, and help us refocus our lives toward You and the living message of the cross. In Christ we pray. Amen.

Hymns

"Freely, Freely"
"Bring Them In"
"Jesus Saves"

Proper 27
Sunday between November 6 and November 12 inclusive

First Lesson: Haggai 1:15b—2:9
Theme: God's promised blessing

Call To Worship

Leader: Give praise to the Lord, for God's kingdom is at hand!

People: But we long for the glory of days now long since past.

Leader: Seek not the past; for the glory of God's Word is abundant for this day.

People: Can the wonder of tomorrow in Christ be greater than what we once knew?

Leader: There is no limit to the depth and splendor of God's eternal kingdom.

All: Blessed be the name of the Lord!

Collect

Almighty and merciful God, even in our times of sorrow You have blessings yet for us to receive. Lord, help us keep our focus on You so we might see the wonders You have planned for us. In Christ we pray. Amen.

Prayer Of Confession

Lord, we have often found ourselves focused and mournful about what is now past and gone forever as we remain stubbornly unwilling even to consider the great things You have in store for Your faithful. Forgive us, Lord, and soften our hearts so we might realize that the greatness of Your tomorrow may well be beyond all we could have ever dreamed or hoped. In Christ we pray. Amen.

Hymns

"My Hope Is Built"
"Be Still, My Soul"
"Just When I Need Him Most"

Proper 27
Sunday between November 6 and November 12 inclusive

Second Lesson: 2 Thessalonians 2:1-5, 13-17
Theme: Standing firm in our faith

Call To Worship
Leader: Come, let all who love Christ gather this day for worship and praise!

People: In Christ is our redemption, and we can worship no other god or power.

Leader: Let our very lives proclaim the glory of the Lord for all to see.

People: We must remain true to our faith in the midst of good times or bad.

Leader: The world will know we serve Christ by the joy and love in our souls.

All: Blessed be the name of the Lord!

Collect
O Lord, You have promised always to be with us if we will only remain true to our faith. Give us the courage and strength to stand firm for You, and the wisdom to know Your will daily. In Christ we pray. Amen.

Prayer Of Confession
Lord, far too often in our lives we have compromised our faith when confronted with the everyday pressures of the world around us. We have yielded when standing firm on our faith could have been a powerful witness to those around us. Forgive us, Lord, and touch our hearts daily so that we might stand true and boldly as witnesses for You. In Christ we pray. Amen.

Hymns
"I'll Go Where You Want Me To Go"
"I Would Be True"
"Are Ye Able?"

191

Proper 27
Sunday between November 6 and November 12 inclusive

Gospel: Luke 20:27-38
Theme: God of the living

Call To Worship

Leader: We are called together this day by the living Lord God Almighty:

People: God Who is with us in our coming and our going;

Leader: God Who is with us in our good times and our times of trouble;

People: God Who is with us in both the days and the nights of life.

Leader: Let us give praise to our gracious, merciful and loving God.

All: Blessed be the name of the Lord!

Collect

O God, in the resurrection You gave us the message that You are indeed the God of the living and we need not fear even death itself. We praise You, O Lord, and give You our love. In Christ we pray. Amen.

Prayer Of Confession

Lord, so many times we speak of the resurrection and of eternity but fail to let their reality touch our lives in the way we live. So often we act as if today is all there is, and we fail to show others the true life You came to give us through the cross. Forgive us, Lord, and help us in faith to move beyond the present and to live toward eternity. In Christ we pray. Amen.

Hymns

"Spirit Of The Living God"
"Christ For The World We Sing"
"He Leadeth Me"

Proper 28
Sunday between November 13 and November 19 inclusive

First Lesson: Isaiah 65:17-25
Theme: God's new earth

Call To Worship

Leader: Let all who seek the Kingdom of the Lord gather now
for worship!

**People: In Christ we have a new spirit fixed not on destruction
but on love.**

Leader: Respect and care for our neighbors will replace fences
and strife.

**People: Seeking good for others around us will replace seek-
ing good only for ourselves.**

Leader: And the praises for God's love will replace the cries of
anguish in life.

All: Blessed be the name of the Lord!

Collect

Most loving and merciful God, in Christ You have called us to
be a part of Your Kingdom, and in it we glimpse Your promised
eternity to come. Help us faithfully to spread the Good News, Lord.
In Christ we pray. Amen.

Prayer Of Confession

Lord, we often forget that You called us into Your Kingdom so
we might live before the world the very message of Christ You
would have us proclaim. Instead we become entangled more in
the hateful ways of the world than we do in the loving lifestyle
You created us to demonstrate. Forgive us, Lord, and call us again
to live for You. In Christ we pray. Amen.

Hymns

"This Is My Father's World"
"God Of The Sparrow"
"Because He Lives"

193

Proper 28
Sunday between November 13 and November 19 inclusive

Second Lesson: 2 Thessalonians 3:6-13
Theme: Christian self-discipline

Call To Worship
Leader: Let our hearts be filled with joy, for we are redeemed Children of God!

People: Our sins have been washed away, yet sin still remains in our hearts.

Leader: In Christ we seek to develop control over the lusts that enter our lives.

People: We must focus on what is necessary, not on the offerings of the world.

Leader: And when we do, the Lord will bless us with contentment, peace, and joy.

All: Blessed be the name of the Lord!

Collect
Almighty and wonderful God, in Your mercy and grace You have called us Your beloved children, leading us ever forward into being more and more Christ-like. Help us resist the sin around us, Lord. In Christ we pray. Amen.

Prayer Of Confession
Lord, far too often we have stumbled and fallen into the very sins we are trying to avoid. Sometimes we even seem to program ourselves to fail by not avoiding the temptations that lead us to sin. Forgive us, Lord, and help us remember Your promise to be with us if only we will seek Your guidance in prayer and battle our sins with all of our being. In Christ we pray. Amen.

Hymns
"Close To Thee"
"Savior, Like A Shepherd Lead Us"
"Nearer, My God, To Thee"

Proper 28
Sunday between November 13 and November 19 inclusive

Gospel: Luke 21:5-19
Theme: Faithful unto the end

Call To Worship

Leader: Let all who await the return of Christ unite today in worship.

People: For Christ is the Lord of history; all nations will bow before God.

Leader: Yet Christ is also the Lord of our hearts and knows each of us well.

People: For the faithful, the final return of the Lord will bring victory.

Leader: And for all who love the Christ there will be eternal life.

All: Blessed be the name of the Lord!

Collect

Almighty and righteous God, be our strength, our courage, and our salvation in the face of all the world might do to silence the message of Your wonderful Good News. In Christ we pray. Amen.

Prayer Of Confession

Lord, as we go through the motions of daily living, we often tend to forget that You will one day hold us accountable for the stewardship of both our lives and the resources You entrusted into our care. Too often we live only for the moment, and we even forget Your promised return. Forgive us, Lord, and help us to live each day dedicated to You. In Christ we pray. Amen.

Hymns

"Abide With Me"
"O God, Our Help In Ages Past"
"I'll Fly Away"

Proper 29 (Christ The King)
Sunday between November 20 and November 26 inclusive

First Lesson: Jeremiah 23:1-6
Theme: God's righteous branch

Call To Worship

Leader: Come now for worship, all who know Christ as your Lord and Savior!

People: Even while we were lost in our sins the Lord sought us to lead us home.

Leader: Many have tried to draw us astray, but the Lord is our loving Shepherd.

People: Our Good Shepherd died so that we might know of God's great redeeming love.

Leader: Christ, the true branch of David's house, offers us eternal life.

All: Blessed be the name of the Lord!

Collect

Almighty and just God, in Christ You sent us the one true and righteous branch through which we may have salvation and eternal life. Lord, give us the strength to share the Good News. In Christ we pray. Amen.

Prayer Of Confession

Lord, we have thought of ourselves as righteous, and yet we have failed to see the sin in our lives. Too often, Lord, when we have fallen short of what You created us to be, we have made up excuses and pleaded like children that "everyone else is doing it." Forgive us, Lord, and help us take responsibility for living our lives as Your faithful servants. In Christ we pray. Amen.

Hymns

"The Lord Is My Shepherd"
"My Faith Looks Up To Thee"
"Praise Him, Praise Him"

Proper 29 (Christ The King)
Sunday between November 20 and November 26 inclusive

Second Lesson: Colossians 1:11-20
Theme: Christ, the fullness of God

Call To Worship

Leader: Come, let us worship the King! Give praise to our Lord Jesus Christ!

People: For in Jesus was our promised Messiah, God with us in every way.

Leader: And all who know Christ know also the very heart of Almighty God.

People: God was in Christ, redeeming us and calling us to receive eternity.

Leader: Let us then celebrate the fullness of God in Christ our blessed Savior.

All: Blessed be the name of the Lord!

Collect

O God, it is staggering to imagine that You walk with us and would commune with us at every chance if we would but come to You. Lord, help us make way for more time in prayer with You. In Christ we pray. Amen.

Prayer Of Confession

Lord, so often we have allowed the daily chores and toils of life to draw us away from spending quality prayer time with You. We have even sought to hide in the activities of the church, rather than make time for You in our lives. Forgive us, Lord, and help us realize the wonderful gift You have given us to share our lives with Almighty God. In Christ we pray. Amen.

Hymns

"Be Thou My Vision"
"Tell Me The Story Of Jesus"
"Majesty"

Proper 29 (Christ The King)
Sunday between November 20 and November 26 inclusive

Gospel: Luke 23:33-43
Theme: We know not what we do!

Call To Worship

Leader: Let all who seek the presence of the Lord come together!

People: Lord, come into our lives and touch our hearts.

Leader: We seek God's guidance in all we would do or say.

People: Lord, come into our lives and open our hearts so that we may know You.

Leader: God so loved us that we were sent the Christ to give us eternal life.

All: **Blessed be the name of the Lord!**

Collect

O God, in the cross we come face to face with all of the hate, sin, and rejection the world could deliver, yet Your love was victorious, and we have salvation. Help us to share it with others. In Christ we pray. Amen.

Prayer Of Confession

Lord, so often we call out for You to be with us, yet we will not open our eyes of faith and see Your presence; or we ask for Your guidance, yet we try to tell You the ways we want to go. Forgive us, Lord, and help us to have the courage to let go of our preconceived ideas so that we might know and accept Your presence in our lives today. In Christ we pray. Amen.

Hymns

"I Know Whom I Have Believed"
"Open My Eyes, That I May See"
"In Christ There Is No East Or West"

All Saints' Day

First Lesson: Daniel 7:1-3, 15-18
Theme: God's kingdom shall endure forever

Call To Worship

Leader: Come, let the saints of the church gather this day for worship!

People: Many of God's saints have gone before us and many are yet to come.

Leader: The saints of God's kingdom will reign with Christ forever.

People: And when the last trumpet sounds our hearts will be filled with joy.

Leader: Then let our voices be raised in praise and song before Almighty God.

All: **Blessed be the name of the Lord!**

Collect

Almighty and gracious God, in Your power and glory Your kingdom will endure forever, and every knee will bow and pay homage to Christ our wonderful king. We praise You, O Lord. In Christ we pray. Amen.

Prayer Of Confession

Lord, sometimes we have been thoughtless as we have failed to remember those who faithfully carried the Gospel through the ages so that we might hear Your Good News and serve You today. Forgive us, Lord, and use us in the same way to carry the Gospel to the generations yet to come so they might also know the joy of Your love in their hearts. In Christ we pray. Amen.

Hymns

"Come, Thou Almighty King"
"There's Something About That Name"
"How Great Thou Art"

All Saints' Day

Second Lesson: Ephesians 1:11-23
Theme: Christ above all names

Call To Worship

Leader: Let us give praise to the Lord for our salvation in Christ Jesus!

People: Only in Christ have we received the blessing of eternal life.

Leader: Above all names is Christ to be praised for showing us God's love.

People: And we are called to share God's love throughout the world.

Leader: Let us join the saints of history in celebrating our salvation in Christ.

All: Blessed be the name of the Lord!

Collect

Most loving and merciful Creator God, so many times You have shown us Your love, and in Christ You call us to join the saints of history in Your Holy service. We thank and praise You, Lord. In Christ we pray. Amen.

Prayer Of Confession

O Lord, so many times in our lives we have allowed the influence of others to come before You. We have allowed almost anything imaginable to be so important to us that it takes Your place and dominates our lives. Forgive us, Lord, and once again help us restore our focus on You and on sharing Your wonderful Good News with all who will listen. In Christ we pray. Amen.

Hymns

"All Hail The Power Of Jesus' Name"
"His Name Is Wonderful"
"O How I Love Jesus"

All Saints' Day

Gospel: Luke 6:20-31
Theme: The dearly beloved in the eyes of God

Call To Worship

Leader: Let us enter the house of the Lord in joyful celebration of God's love!

People: But we are not all of wealth and we do not have the fine things of life.

Leader: The poor and afflicted are especially beloved in the eyes of the Lord.

People: Are all welcome before the throne of Almighty God?

Leader: All who love God and who hear the cries of the poor and the needy are welcome.

All: Blessed be the name of the Lord!

Collect

Most loving and merciful God, in Christ You called all who would be Your saints to be about the work of caring for the sick and helping the poor and needy. Guide us daily to serve You, Lord. In Christ we pray. Amen.

Prayer Of Confession

Lord, so often we have believed more in our personal comfort than in Your Word or the way You lived Your life. We have allowed ourselves to look down on the poor or disadvantaged, yet You spent much of Your earthly ministry tending to their needs. Forgive us, Lord, and call us again to join Your saints in caring for those in need. In Christ we pray. Amen.

Hymns

"Jesus Loves Me"
"Love Divine, All Loves Excelling"
"I'm A Child Of The King"

Thanksgiving Day

First Lesson: Deuteronomy 26:1-11
Theme: Give praise and thanksgiving for God's blessings

Call To Worship

Leader: Let us give praise and thanksgiving for the wonderful blessings of God!

People: God is our salvation and sustains us, even amid the storms of life.

Leader: Sing with great joy and celebration, for the Lord has blessed us each one.

People: We have each been blessed in God's wonderful love and grace.

Leader: We were but sinners, yet God redeemed us and called us to bless the world!

All: Blessed be the name of the Lord!

Collect

Almighty God, You would certainly have been justified to have held us to account for each and every sin in our lives, yet You chose in Christ to forgive and bless us. We praise You, Lord. In Christ we pray. Amen.

Prayer Of Confession

Lord, we have taken Your wonderful blessings for granted and at times have felt that we really deserved them. We have failed to understand that Your blessings are meant to be passed on and shared as a witness to Your mercy and grace. Forgive us, Lord, and make of us blessings in the world today so that all may know that You are truly the Lord God. In Christ we pray. Amen.

Hymns

"Come, Ye Thankful People, Come"
"Count Your Blessings"
"Praise To The Lord, The Almighty"

Thanksgiving Day

Second Lesson: Philippians 4:4-9
Theme: "Rejoice in the Lord always" (RSV)

Call To Worship

Leader: Let us give praise to the Lord God Almighty on this day
of Thanksgiving!

**People: God has been with us and blessed us even in ways we
do not yet know.**

Leader: The Lord is our Savior and our guide through the perils
of sin and death.

**People: The Lord is our Good Shepherd, who cares for and
protects us in life.**

Leader: The Lord our God is great and worthy to receive our
praise!

All: Blessed be the name of the Lord!

Collect

Almighty and loving God, in our wildest imagination we could
not have thought of the depth of Your love for us. We give You our
heartfelt thanks and praise for the love You first showed us. In
Christ we pray. Amen.

Prayer Of Confession

Lord, so often we have allowed the ways of the world to come
before Your claim on our hearts. We have even accepted Your
blessings and yet failed to stop even for a moment to express our
gratitude. Forgive us, Lord, and call us again into Your faithful
service and bless our efforts to share the Good News of salvation
in Christ with others. In Christ we pray. Amen.

Hymns

"For The Beauty Of The Earth"
"Great Is Thy Faithfulness"
"Rejoice, Ye Pure In Heart"

Thanksgiving Day

Gospel: John 6:25-35
Theme: Christ is the Bread of Life

Call To Worship

Leader: Come, let us lift our grateful praise for the bounty of the Lord!

People: Christ is the true Bread of Life, and in Christ we have life eternal.

Leader: Then let our voices ring out in wonderful thanksgiving to God!

People: Praise be to the Lord who went to the cross so we could have life itself!

Leader: Praise be to the Lord who is the author of our glorious salvation!

All: Blessed be the name of the Lord!

Collect

Almighty and merciful God, in Christ You have taught us the true self-sacrificing nature of love, and You have called us to live and share it wherever we go. We praise You, O Lord. In Christ we pray. Amen.

Prayer Of Confession

O God, as we gather today to give thanks for Your blessings, our hearts are touched by all of those times when You called us to be loving witnesses for You and we would not respond. You died for our sins, yet so often we would not even bother to share Your mercy and grace with others. Forgive us, Lord, and call us again to be living witnesses of Your divine love today. In Christ we pray. Amen.

Hymns

"Now Thank We All Our God"
"This Is My Father's World"
"To God Be The Glory"

Martin Luther King, Jr., Sunday

Scripture: Matthew 5:9
Theme: Blessed are the peacemakers

Call To Worship

Leader: Let all who would seek God's holy peace come together this day!

People: For there are storms of hate and controversy swirling all around us.

Leader: Yet the children of God are called to proclaim truth and justice.

People: But there are forces in the world that speak only through violence.

Leader: Yet God's eternal peace is greater by far than any worldly force.

All: Blessed be the name of the Lord!

Collect

O God, Lord of justice and truth, we seek Your strength and guidance that we might be among Your saints struggling to bring freedom and justice to all of Your children. In Christ we pray. Amen.

Prayer Of Confession

Lord, You send Your prophets and Your peacemakers so we might know Your will for all people to be loved and respected, but we do not hear. You give us great leaders to show us Your way, but so often we are not willing to follow. You call us to be Your forgiving Church but we will not forgive. Forgive us now, Lord, and call us anew to serve. In Christ we pray. Amen.

Hymns

"Let There Be Peace On Earth"
"O God Of Every Nation"
"We Shall Overcome"

*Parent's Days

Scripture: Luke 2:41-52
Theme: Praise for the blessing of parents

Call To Worship

Leader: Let us come together giving honor to Almighty God!

People: Let us honor those who led us in the ways of the Lord in our youth!

Leader: Praise be to God for the families we shared in our childhood!

People: Praise be to the Lord that we are adopted into the family of God!

Leader: May the Lord bless the loved ones of our youth wherever they may be.

All: Blessed be the name of the Lord!

Collect

O God, in Your infinite wisdom You have blessed us with families. Just as we love and honor You, O God, we love and honor the parents of our childhood. We give You our praise, Lord. In Christ we pray. Amen.

Prayer Of Confession

Lord, so often we have taken for granted the help and guidance You have given us through our families. And so often, Lord, we have failed to hear Your voice calling us to share Your love with all around us and to be Your family for a hurting world. Forgive us, Lord, and help us carry Your loving mercy and grace wherever we go. In Christ we pray. Amen.

Hymns

"Happy The Home When God Is There"
"O Lord, May Church And Home Combine"
"Blest Be The Tie"

*May be used for Mother's Day and/or Father's Day

Fourth Of July

Scripture: Genesis 12:1-8; John 8:31-36
Theme: A blessed nation

Call To Worship

Leader: Let us gather this day for worship as a nation truly blessed by God.

People: Many fine people have given their lives that we might be free.

Leader: And many have defended liberty and justice for all around the world.

People: Yet if we are to remain free we must be willing to protect liberty.

Leader: And if we are to remain free we must be true to the Lord our God.

All: Blessed be the name of the Lord!

Collect

O God, our Almighty Defender and Shield, we lift our voices in praise to You for the many blessings You have so freely given to us. Use our nation in Your mighty kingdom. In Christ we pray. Amen.

Prayer Of Confession

Lord, so often as we live our everyday lives, we fail to appreciate the wonderful ways in which You have so blessed our nation. Too often, Lord, we have taken for granted even the basic freedoms others, in less fortunate nations, only dream of one day having. Forgive us, Lord, and lead us into ways we can share Your blessings with the world. In Christ we pray. Amen.

Hymns

"America The Beautiful"
"My Country, 'Tis Of Thee"
"God Of The Ages"

World-wide Communion Sunday

Scripture: Acts 10:23b-48
Theme: We are one in Christ

Call To Worship

Leader: Come! Let all who are one in the body of Christ gather for worship!

People: Whether we are great or small, rich or poor, free or bondslave,

Leader: We are each united, one with each other, through the love of Christ.

People: This day Christians in every land will gather together for worship.

Leader: And in the holy meal of Christ they will again declare God's love.

All: Blessed be the name of the Lord!

Collect

O God, we have feelings of wonder when we realize Christians around the world in every land will be united celebrating Holy Communion this day together. Lord, we give You our praise. In Christ we pray. Amen.

Prayer Of Confession

Lord, so often we think only in terms of our separate congregations and we fail to realize we are all, in Christ, united as a part of the Church Universal. Forgive us, Lord, and help us to reach out and celebrate the things we share in common rather than divide over the differences we may have with other Christians. Unite us in Your love, Lord. In Christ we pray. Amen.

Hymns

"Break Thou The Bread Of Life"
"Let Us Break Bread Together"
"We Are One In The Spirit"

Scripture Index

A Note Concerning Lectionaries And Calendars

The following index will aid the user of this book in matching the correct Sunday with the appropriate text during Pentecost. During the Pentecost season, this book lists Sundays by Proper (following the Revised Common and Episcopal lectionary system). Lutheran and Roman Catholic designations indicate days comparable to Sundays on which the Propers are used.

(Fixed dates do not pertain to Lutheran Lectionary)

Fixed Date Lectionaries *Revised Common (including ELCA)* *and Roman Catholic*	Lutheran Lectionary *Lutheran*
The Day of Pentecost	The Day of Pentecost
The Holy Trinity	The Holy Trinity
May 29-June 4 — Proper 4, Ordinary Time 9	Pentecost 2
June 5-11 — Proper 5, Ordinary Time 10	Pentecost 3
June 12-18 — Proper 6, Ordinary Time 11	Pentecost 4
June 19-25 — Proper 7, Ordinary Time 12	Pentecost 5
June 26-July 2 — Proper 8, Ordinary Time 13	Pentecost 6
July 3-9 — Proper 9, Ordinary Time 14	Pentecost 7
July 10-16 — Proper 10, Ordinary Time 15	Pentecost 8
July 17-23 — Proper 11, Ordinary Time 16	Pentecost 9
July 24-30 — Proper 12, Ordinary Time 17	Pentecost 10
July 31-Aug. 6 — Proper 13, Ordinary Time 18	Pentecost 11
Aug. 7-13 — Proper 14, Ordinary Time 19	Pentecost 12
Aug. 14-20 — Proper 15, Ordinary Time 20	Pentecost 13
Aug. 21-27 — Proper 16, Ordinary Time 21	Pentecost 14
Aug. 28-Sept. 3 — Proper 17, Ordinary Time 22	Pentecost 15
Sept. 4-10 — Proper 18, Ordinary Time 23	Pentecost 16

Sept. 11-17 — Proper 19, Ordinary Time 24	Pentecost 17
Sept. 18-24 — Proper 20, Ordinary Time 25	Pentecost 18
Sept. 25-Oct. 1 — Proper 21, Ordinary Time 26	Pentecost 19
Oct. 2-8 — Proper 22, Ordinary Time 27	Pentecost 20
Oct. 9-15 — Proper 23, Ordinary Time 28	Pentecost 21
Oct. 16-22 — Proper 24, Ordinary Time 29	Pentecost 22
Oct. 23-29 — Proper 25, Ordinary Time 30	Pentecost 23
Oct. 30-Nov. 5 — Proper 26, Ordinary Time 31	Pentecost 24
Nov. 6-12 — Proper 27, Ordinary Time 32	Pentecost 25
Nov. 13-19 — Proper 28, Ordinary Time 33	Pentecost 26
	Pentecost 27
Nov. 20-26 — Christ the King	Christ the King

Reformation Day (or last Sunday in October) is October 31 (Revised Common, Lutheran)

All Saints' Day (or first Sunday in November) is November 1 (Revised Common, Lutheran, Roman Catholic)